PHYSICS IN
OUR WORLD

TIME and
THERMODYNAMICS

Kyle Kirkland, Ph.D.

Facts On File

An imprint of Infobase Publishing

TIME AND THERMODYNAMICS

Facts On File, Inc.
An imprint of Infobase Publishing
132 West 31st Street
New York NY 10001

ISBN-10: 0-8160-6113-0
ISBN-13: 978-0-8160-6113-6

Library of Congress Cataloging-in-Publication Data

Kirkland, Kyle.
   Time and thermodynamics / Kyle Kirkland.
      p. cm.—(Physics in our world)
   Includes bibliographical references and index.
   ISBN 0-8160-6113-0
1. Thermodynamics. 2. Space and time. 3. Heat. 4. Temperature. I. Title. II. Series.
   QC311.K56 2007
   536'.7—dc22   2006016638

Facts On File books are available at special discounts when purchased in bulk quantities for businesses, associations, institutions, or sales promotions. Please call our Special Sales Department in New York at (212) 967-8800 or (800) 322-8755.

You can find Facts On File on the World Wide Web at http://www.factsonfile.com

Text design and composition by Kerry Casey
Cover design by Dorothy M. Preston
Illustrations by Richard Garratt
Cover printed by Maple Press, York, PA
Book printed and bound by Maple Press, York, PA
Date printed: October 2010
Printed in the United States of America

10 9 8 7 6 5 4 3 2

This book is printed on acid-free paper.

❄ CONTENTS ❄

Preface	v
Acknowledgments	vii
Introduction	ix

1 HEAT AND THE ENVIRONMENT — 1

Temperature and Heat	2
Temperature and the Kinetic Energy of Molecules	*4*
The Flow of Energy	8
Cooling Down and Heating Up	14
Latent Heats and Heat Capacity	*16*
Seasons of the Year	19
Urban Heat Islands	23
Global Warming	26

2 HEAT AND BODY TEMPERATURE — 31

Body Temperature	32
How People Sense Hot and Cold	35
Heat Conductors and Insulators	*36*
Warm-Blooded and Cold-Blooded Animals	39
The Comfort Zone: Maintaining the Right Temperature	42
Thermography	47
Extreme Temperatures and Life	49

3 HEAT AND TECHNOLOGY — 55

Using Technology to Control Temperature	56
First Law of Thermodynamics	*57*

Refrigerators and Air Conditioners 60

Second Law of Thermodynamics 62

Reversible Heat Pumps 65

Absolute Zero 67

4 HEAT ENGINES 71

Steam Power 72

The Carnot Engine 78

Car Engines 82

Racing Engines 88

Jet Engines and Gas Turbines 92

Heat Engines of the Future 96

5 TIME 101

Clocks 102

Pendulums and Periodicity 106

Time and the Laws of Physics 110

Entropy and Disorder 114

Second Law of Thermodynamics Revisited 117

Traveling in Time 118

The Beginning and the End of the Universe 122

CONCLUSION 125

SI Units and Conversions 129

Glossary 132

Further Reading and Web Sites 136

Index 141

✤ PREFACE ✤

THE NUCLEAR BOMBS that ended World War II in 1945 were a convincing and frightening demonstration of the power of physics. A product of some of the best scientific minds in the world, the nuclear explosions devastated the Japanese cities of Hiroshima and Nagasaki, forcing Japan into an unconditional surrender. But even though the atomic bomb was the most dramatic example, physics and physicists made their presence felt throughout World War II. From dam-breaking bombs that skipped along the water to submerged mines that exploded when they magnetically sensed the presence of a ship's hull, the war was as much a scientific struggle as anything else.

World War II convinced everyone, including skeptical military leaders, that physics is an essential science. Yet the reach of this subject extends far beyond military applications. The principles of physics affect every part of the world and touch on all aspects of people's lives. Hurricanes, lightning, automobile engines, eyeglasses, skyscrapers, footballs, and even the way people walk and run must follow the dictates of scientific laws.

The relevance of physics in everyday life has often been overshadowed by topics such as nuclear weapons or the latest theories of how the universe began. Physics in Our World is a set of volumes that aims to explore the whole spectrum of applications, describing how physics influences technology and society, as well as helping people understand the nature and behavior of the universe and all its many interacting parts. The set covers the major branches of physics and includes the following titles:

- ♦ *Force and Motion*
- ♦ *Electricity and Magnetism*

- *Time and Thermodynamics*
- *Light and Optics*
- *Atoms and Materials*
- *Particles and the Universe*

Each volume explains the basic concepts of the subject and then discusses a variety of applications in which these concepts apply. Although physics is a mathematical subject, the focus of these books is on the ideas rather than the mathematics. Only simple equations are included. The reader does not need any special knowledge of mathematics, although an understanding of elementary algebra would be helpful in a few cases. The number of possible topics for each volume is practically limitless, but there is only room for a sample; regrettably, interesting applications had to be omitted. But each volume in the set explores a wide range of material, and all volumes contain a further reading and Web sites section that lists a selection of books and Web sites for continued exploration. This selection is also only a sample, offering suggestions of the many exploration opportunities available.

I was once at a conference in which a young student asked a group of professors whether he needed the latest edition of a physics textbook. One professor replied no, because the principles of physics "have not changed in years." This is true for the most part, but it is a testament to the power of physics. Another testament to physics is the astounding number of applications relying on these principles—and these applications continue to expand and change at an exceptionally rapid pace. Steam engines have yielded to the powerful internal combustion engines of race cars and fighter jets, and telephone wires are in the process of yielding to fiber optics, satellite communication, and cell phones. The goal of these books is to encourage the reader to see the relevance of physics in all directions and in every endeavor, at the present time as well as in the past and in the years to come.

❋ ACKNOWLEDGMENTS ❋

THANKS GO TO my teachers, many of whom did their best to put up with me and my undisciplined ways. Special thanks go to Drs. George Gerstein, Larry Palmer, and Stanley Schmidt for helping me find my way when I got lost. I also much appreciate the contributions of Jodie Rhodes, who helped launch this project; executive editor Frank K. Darmstadt and the editorial and production teams who pushed it along, including copy editor Amy L. Conver; and the many scientists, educators, and writers who provided some of their time and insight. Thanks most of all go to Elizabeth Kirkland, a super mom with extraordinary powers and a gift for using them wisely.

❋ INTRODUCTION ❋

A LEGEND OF the ancient Greeks tells the story of a god called Prometheus, who taught people how to make fire. This gave a tremendous boost to humanity, and the other gods were furious with Prometheus for allowing humans to wield such potency.

Although the story of Prometheus is a myth, the ability to harness fire and *heat* did provide people with some of their earliest technology. Steam powered much of the Industrial Revolution, a period of time beginning in the late 18th century in which machines tremendously advanced the productivity of manufacturing and transportation. But heat, *temperature,* and their relationships are much broader subjects than just steam-powered machines. Warmth is associated with life and activity; cold is associated with death and stillness. Some organisms rely on the environment to provide warmth, and some organisms can generate their own, but all living beings must adapt and interact in a world in which temperature is not constant.

Time and Thermodynamics explores the physics of heat and temperature and their effects on people's lives and technology. The word *thermo* refers to heat, and the word *dynamics* gives an indication of motion, both of which are vital to the subject. Heat is *energy* that flows from warm objects to cooler ones. Nineteenth-century scientists and engineers such as Sadi Carnot, primarily motivated by the desire to understand and improve steam-powered machines, discovered the principles of *thermodynamics.* Much to their surprise, they found that the physics of thermodynamics places strict limits on what machines can accomplish. But the subject also opened up vast areas of knowledge in habitats, biology, technology, engines, as well as a surprising amount of revelation on the topic of time. *Time and Thermodynamics* discusses thermodynamics principles related to each of these topics and how their application enables people to better understand the world and sometimes even improve it.

Temperature is vital to the health and welfare of all animals, and Earth's temperature varies considerably from place to place. Early humans could only live in warm areas such as the tropics, near the equator. Although modern humans have the technology to keep their houses and offices warm even in cold environments, the growth and development of civilization has created unintentional effects. Cities are warmer than their surrounding regions, and on a global scale, Earth is experiencing rising temperatures. Thermodynamics offers an important tool to study these effects.

Maintaining proper temperature is critical for life, and this need has a great influence on the form, function, and molecules of the bodies and organs of people and animals. Reptiles bask in the sun for warmth, but humans generate a lot of heat on their own. These two methods of keeping warm differ in significant ways, yet both adhere to thermodynamic principles of heat generation and transfer.

Heat naturally flows from warm to cold objects, but it is often desirable to get it to go in the opposite direction. Air conditioners pump heat from the inside of a relatively cool house to the hot environment outside on a summer day. The process requires energy, usually taken from electricity, and the reason why strikes at the heart of the laws of thermodynamics.

Thermodynamics laws also put strict limits on the ability of engines to use heat to propel vehicles or raise heavy objects. Knowing these limits prevents engineers from trying to design impossible machines, but it does not stop them from building impressive cars capable of roaring down a racetrack at 200 miles per hour (320 km/hr.), jet fighters that exceed the speed of sound by a factor of two or three, and a new engine called a ramjet to accelerate an aircraft up to 7,000 miles per hour (11,200 km/hr.).

The final chapter explores time. Although time would not seem at first to have strong ties with thermodynamics, the relationship is profound. Physics has much symmetry—the laws of physics are often the same in a variety of circumstances. This includes time; physics formulas are usually the same whether time is increasing (going forward, into the future) or decreasing (going backward, into the past). Most of physics has no preference for either case, because its laws work equally well in both directions. Yet people experience time as flowing in a single direction, from past to present and on into the future. Thermodynamics provides an ingenious explanation for this, because its laws are an exception to the rest of physics and breaks the symmetry in time. As a result, thermodynamics yields clues about the nature of time, the possibility of time travel, and the very beginning of time, at the creation of the universe.

1

HEAT AND THE ENVIRONMENT

A GIGANTIC ICEBERG floating in the ocean is frigid, yet it has a lot of *thermal energy*. The word *thermal* is derived from a Greek word meaning heat. The iceberg is not hot, but it contains a lot of thermal energy.

This strange-looking iceberg was floating in the Gerlache Strait near Antarctica in 1962. *(NOAA/Rear Admiral Harley D. Nygren)*

Thermodynamics is the study of heat and its relation to other forms of energy. The word *heat,* in its everyday usage, does not generally refer to energy—people use the terms *hot* and *cold* to describe how something feels to the touch, and heating an object means raising its temperature. A sidewalk on a summer day is hot, and an ice cube is cold. Most people tend to think about temperature rather than energy.

But the physics of thermodynamics is all about energy. Physicists define energy as the ability to do *work*—the application of a force to move an object, such as pushing a cart or throwing a football. Energy is strongly related to motion, or at least the capacity to move, and thermal energy—heat—is no exception. Thermal energy is everywhere, even in icebergs, and its properties, especially the way it moves from one object to another, affects people whether they live in the tropics, the North Pole, or the mild climate of a coastal community. The principles of thermodynamics are critical in the changes marking the seasons of the year, the weather differences between city and countryside, and a worldwide trend toward warmer temperatures.

Temperature and Heat

In physics, there is a big difference between temperature and heat. Although it is not at all obvious, temperature is related to the energy of the atoms and molecules of an object. Heat is the energy that flows from one body to another when there is a difference between their temperatures.

People used to think heat was a *fluid* that flowed from hot objects to cold ones. But this is not true, as discovered by physicist and politician Benjamin Thompson (1752–1814), who was also known as Count Rumford. In the 1790s, Count Rumford studied the process by which workers drilled a hole in a solid brass cylinder to make a cannon. One day he submerged the steel drill and brass cylinder underwater, and as the hole was drilled, the water got hot enough to boil. The water kept boiling as long as the drilling continued, which was a strange occurrence if heat was indeed a fluid—surely the metal would run out of the fluid sooner or later, yet it never did. Another important observation was that the weight of the cannon plus the shavings (removed by the drilling process) did not change, even though a change would have been expected if the metal had lost a lot of fluid.

Rumford realized that the water's temperature was rising not because of a flow of fluid but because of the motion of the drill. Heat is not a fluid; heat is energy flowing from one object to another. Although Rumford could not grasp all the details, he observed that the *friction* of the drill bit against the cylinder wall was causing the rise in temperature.

Heat is strongly related to motion, as suggested by processes involving friction—the rubbing of one object against another. Friction generates higher temperatures, and people rub their hands together on a cold day to warm them up.

But heat and temperature are related to motion on an even more fundamental level. All objects are made of atoms and molecules—tiny pieces of matter so small that they cannot be seen with the eye, or even in microscopes. Atoms and molecules are never at rest—they are always in motion. This is especially true of the form of matter called a gas, as shown in the figure below, but it is true of liquids and solids as well. An object's temperature is a

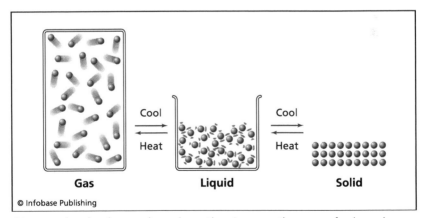

© Infobase Publishing

Atoms and molecules are always in motion. In a gas, they move freely, and in a liquid, they jostle their neighbors. The particles in most solids are at fixed positions, but they move a tiny distance back and forth about their position.

Temperature and the Kinetic Energy of Molecules

Human sensation of temperature in terms of hot and cold is useful, but temperature also happens to be a measure of the motion of an object's particles. In a gas, the particles are free to roam about, and this motion is easy to visualize. Although atoms and molecules are not normally visible, several methods can measure their motion. One method for a gas is to allow some of the particles to escape the container through a small hole. The escaped particles pass through a series of rotating wheels, which are solid except for gaps at specific places. Only particles having a specific speed will pass through all the wheels, and the rest of the particles will be blocked. This action is somewhat like a car passing through a series of traffic lights—a car traveling at the right speed will hit all the traffic lights while they are green, but other cars will get stopped by a red light somewhere along the route. By repeating the experiment a number of times for a gas at a specific temperature, an experimenter can measure the range of speeds of the particles.

The faster the particles in a substance move, the higher the temperature. Although a few particles in a cold gas can be moving extremely fast, it is the average that matters. On average, particles of a cold gas are moving more slowly than a hot one.

In a liquid or a solid, there is internal motion—movement of the particles—but this motion is more complicated. The atoms and molecules of a liquid are pushed together, but they are free to slide over and around one another. In solids such as crystals, the atoms and molecules form a rigid geometrical structure, yet the particles are not at rest—they vibrate, moving back and forth about some central position, similar to the motion of a swinging *pendulum*.

measure of the average *kinetic energy*—motion—of the atoms and molecules that compose it, as discussed in the sidebar.

The energy possessed by the atoms and molecules of an object is sometimes called its internal energy or its thermal energy. All objects contain this energy, even ones people regard as cold. An iceberg floating in the Arctic Ocean is cold, but it is massive, and so despite the fact that its atoms and molecules do not move very much, there are so many of them that the iceberg contains quite a bit of energy. There is enough energy to warm a house for weeks, if that energy could somehow be extracted. But the problem is that the laws of thermodynamics, described later, are not very generous when it comes to extracting energy from cold objects.

Despite the relation between internal motion and temperature, most people do not measure an object's temperature by some kind of elaborate process to analyze the motion of atoms and molecules. Instead they use a *thermometer*.

Old-fashioned thermometers, called analog thermometers, were based on the properties of mercury or alcohol. As a substance such as mercury gets hotter, its constituent atoms and molecules begin moving around a lot more. As a result, the substance normally expands—it gets slightly larger. This is called *thermal expansion*. The mercury's atoms are always jiggling around, but heat makes them jiggle more because of the added energy. As the volume of the liquid increases, the mercury rises in the tube. As mercury gets colder, the opposite situation occurs, and its volume falls. The volume of mercury in the tube is an indication of its temperature.

Digital thermometers, which show the temperature as digits on a screen or display, usually measure temperature in other ways. They may measure the thermal expansion of a small piece of metal by carefully monitoring some of the properties that depend on volume, such as the metal's electrical resistance. Some thermometers make use of the different rates that different materials will undergo thermal expansion, as shown in the figure on page 6.

Another way of measuring temperature occurs if an object is hot enough to visibly glow, such as the heating element of an oven or a metal poker that has been left in a fire. The color of a glowing object is related to its temperature: as the temperature rises, the object is first red and then orange, and finally it gets white (or bluish white), the "hottest" color. (This explains the phrase "white hot" when describing something that is very hot.)

The relation between temperature and the color of a glowing object is useful to astronomers. The color of stars is related to their temperature, and since people cannot as yet travel the great

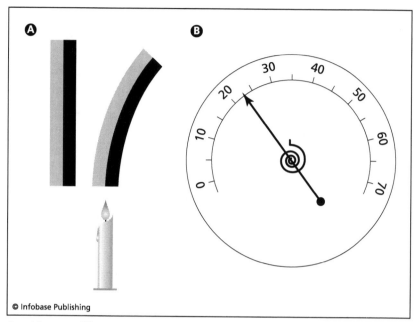

© Infobase Publishing

Consider two different materials glued together in a strip. Different materials usually expand at different rates with an increase in temperature, and as the glued combination gets warm, one of the materials expands a little more than the other. This causes the strip to bend. In the strip illustrated here (A), the white strip expands more than the dark one but is pulled to one side because the shorter material holds it back. The amount of bend depends on temperature (B), making a useful thermometer, especially if the strip is elongated into a spiral shape.

distances to the stars and measure their temperature in a more precise way, astronomers rely on their color. This temperature is of the surface of the star, the part of the star which is emitting the light that can be seen. The interior of the star is at a much higher temperature, though it is concealed. But the information obtained from the color of the star is still useful. Blue stars have surface temperatures much higher than red stars, and the Sun's surface temperature lies between these two.

Like any measurement, temperature is scaled into units, and several different temperature scales exist. The most common scales are Celsius (°C), Fahrenheit (°F), and *Kelvin* or *absolute scale* (K), named after Anders Celsius, Gabriel Fahrenheit, and William Thomson (Lord Kelvin), respectively, who first developed them.

Fahrenheit is commonly used in the United States, while most of the rest of the world uses Celsius.

The Fahrenheit and Celsius scales are based on two temperatures, the freezing point and the boiling point of water. In the Fahrenheit scale, these two temperatures are defined as 32 and 212, respectively; in Celsius, they are 0 and 100. (Because air pressure and therefore altitude affect these points, the defining temperatures refer to the boiling and freezing points of water at sea level.) The numbers are arbitrary, since any two numbers could have been used. But once chosen, the two numbers provide a scale that determines the size of the units, called degrees. There are 212 − 32 = 180 degrees between the boiling and freezing points of water in the Fahrenheit scale, and 100 in the Celsius scale. (Celsius is sometimes called "centigrade" to reflect the fact that it is based on 100.) A degree in the Fahrenheit scale is clearly not equal to a degree in the Celsius scale, and the relation between the two scales is given by the equation

$$T_{Fahrenheit} = 1.8 T_{Celsius} + 32.$$

In the Kelvin, or absolute temperature scale, the size of the unit is taken to be the same as in the Celsius scale. Boiling water (at sea level) is 100 units hotter than freezing water in both the Celsius and absolute scale. But in the absolute scale, the freezing point of water is 273.15, and the boiling point is 373.15. These numbers might seem to be strange choices, but the absolute scale's numbers are based on the existence of the coldest temperature. No object can get any colder than this temperature, which is known as *absolute zero*. This temperature is the "0" in the absolute scale. The selection of this temperature as zero determined all the other values in the scale, including the freezing and boiling point of water, because the size of the unit, called a Kelvin, was already chosen to be equal to the Celsius degree.

It seems reasonable that there is such a thing as a lowest temperature. If temperature is a measure of the motion of atoms and molecules, then an absence of motion would appear to be the coldest possible temperature. But it is not quite as simple as that. Instead of an absence of motion, absolute zero is the minimum amount of motion. The reason that absolute zero corresponds to a minimum (nonzero) motion rather than zero motion is a result of quantum mechanics, which governs the motion of atoms and molecules. Although many of the concepts in quantum mechanics sound odd, experiments support the theory, and quantum mechanics states that no particle can be perfectly still. The thermodynamics of absolute zero is discussed further in chapter 3 of this book.

Thanks to the temperature scale, people can quantify any temperature and compare the temperatures of different objects. The temperature of an oven may be set at a precise 450°F (232.2°C), which is quite a bit warmer than the boiling point of water. The temperature of a January day in Canada may be –13°F (–25°C), which will definitely freeze a glass of water in a hurry. The temperature of the surface of the Sun is about 10,500°F (5,815°C). The temperature of the star's interior—which can at present only be hypothetically calculated, since it cannot be measured directly—is about 27,000,000°F (15,000,000°C).

The Flow of Energy

Heat is energy flowing between objects, detected as far as human senses are concerned by warm or cold perceptions. Energy flows from a warm body to a cold one (or at least a body that is not quite as warm), which can be observed if a hot beverage is poured into a cool glass—the glass gets warmer, and the beverage cools down. The underlying physics of the process is that the atoms and molecules of the warm body transfer some of their energy to the atoms and molecules of the cold body.

There are three ways that the atomic and molecular motion of a warm body can impart some motion onto the atoms and molecules of a cooler body. These are called the mechanisms of *heat transfer*. All of them affect people's lives every minute of every day.

The simplest mechanism of heat transfer is called *conduction*. If one object is touching another, the particles of one object are close enough to jostle those of the other. The particles of the object with the higher temperature are moving faster, and when these quicker molecules bump into the particles of the cooler object, then they start moving faster.

Convection is another heat transfer process. It is similar to conduction, except the energy transfers not from direct contact of the two objects but through an intermediary—something that comes between the two objects and can flow, acting like a carrier. The carrier is a fluid, often air. Currents of air can pick up some of the energy from one object and carry it away. These are called convection currents.

The third mechanism is a little more complex. It is related to the fact that very hot objects can glow, emitting visible light. But not just hot objects glow—all objects glow. That is, all objects give off energy in the form of electromagnetic *radiation*, of which one type is visible light.

The glow coming from most objects is not easy to detect because only hot objects emit electromagnetic radiation that is visible. Cooler objects emit radiation that is not as energetic as

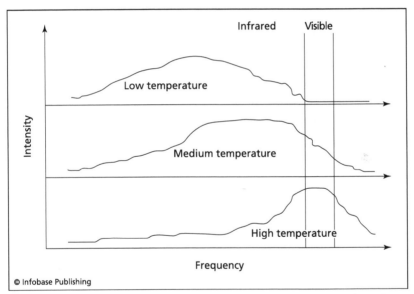

All objects emit radiation, but the frequencies vary with temperature. These three graphs show the intensity (amount) of radiation at a range of frequencies. At low temperatures—on a frigid winter day, for example—objects emit radiation at frequencies well below visible light. At medium temperatures, objects emit more infrared and perhaps a little visible light, and they start to glow. Hot objects such as the cooking elements in an oven emit much light as well as infrared.

visible light and that people cannot directly observe. The bulk of the radiation emitted by such objects is called *infrared radiation*—infrared because its energy is less than or below that of red light (infra means below), which is the lowest-energy radiation people can see. The figure on page 9 shows the differences in the *frequency* of radiation emitted by objects at low, medium, and high temperatures.

Radiation transfers energy because all objects emit radiation, and warmer objects are emitting more energy than cold ones. But radiation is not only emitted, it is also absorbed; because of this, people can feel the Sun's rays warm them as they lay on the beach on a sunny day.

Conduction is not only the simplest mechanism of heat transfer, but it is also probably the best known. Touching a hot stove or the surface of a car after it has been out in the sunlight for a long time is a bad idea, for both the stove and the car will transfer an uncomfortable amount of energy into a hand by conduction.

But not all materials are good *conductors* of heat. Metals are some of the best conductors; if a person is holding a metal wire in contact with a flame or a hot object, it is not long before he or she says "Ouch!" and drops the wire. Materials that do not conduct

These people are enjoying the Sun's rays at a beach in Brazil. *(Elizabeth Kirkland)*

heat very well are called *thermal insulators.* Glass, for instance, is not a good conductor of heat. A substance called asbestos is also a poor thermal conductor and, consequently, is an excellent thermal insulator. (Asbestos was commonly used for insulation and fireproofing until people discovered this material posed a health hazard.) A person can hold an insulator in contact with a hot object much longer than he or she can hold a conductor such as a metal wire.

One of the best thermal insulators is air. This is well known by Eskimos, who protect themselves from the cold by building igloos. The snow used to make the igloo contains a lot of trapped air, which acts as insulation and prevents the heat of the interior from escaping. A material called Styrofoam is a thermal insulator that acts in a similar way—this lightweight material contains a lot of trapped air.

But air can also carry convection currents. Igloos and Styrofoam work as insulators because the air is trapped, so it does not move around much. Air that has room to travel is not insulating. Thermally insulating windows on a house often have an air gap that acts as insulation, but the gap must be small, otherwise convection would defeat the purpose. Researchers have found materials to fill this gap and prevent almost all air current, making these windows even better insulators. One such substance is aerogel, consisting of fine layers of a powdery material.

Heat transfer is also critical for motorists to consider. Drivers crossing bridges in the winter have to be careful because bridges are among the first surfaces to freeze in cold weather. Bridges can be icy even if other paved surfaces are not, and the reason is due to heat transfer. Contact with the warm ground supplies the street pavement with a steady source of heat, but the cold atmosphere, along with convection currents created by winds, carry heat away from elevated surfaces such as bridges.

The heat carried by convection currents can be felt easily enough. Air over a stove warms an outstretched hand. (The hot air rises because it is less dense than the surrounding, colder air.) Convection currents are also important in water. A bathtub full of cold water will not get uniformly warm by turning on the

The Benjamin Franklin Bridge, finished in 1926, connects Philadelphia, Pennsylvania, to Camden, New Jersey, across the Delaware River. *(Kyle Kirkland)*

hot water tap, at least not for quite a while—heat does not travel quickly from the hot water near the spigot to the cooler water near the back (where the bather usually sits). The water needs to be mixed—some convection currents are in order, produced by the bather's hand gently swirling the water.

Radiational heat losses are not so easy to detect. Soldiers fighting at night often wear infrared goggles that give them "night vision." The goggles detect infrared radiation, and the soldiers can see warm objects such as enemy soldiers. But under normal circumstances, radiation fails to be noticed, as few people walk around with infrared goggles. Babies can lose a lot of heat from radiation, even though they are surrounded by warm air. The heat is exchanged with the cold walls of the nursery, and so a warm baby will lose heat unless the child is wrapped in a blanket. Children are always more susceptible to radiational cooling because they are small and have more surface area for their weight than adults. The surface areas emit radiation into the environment, and a larger surface area means more energy will be radiated.

Infrared images tend to be grainy, like this one, but offer vision even in dim light. This image is from a rescue operation for survivors of an Egyptian ferry accident and shows a ship and a life raft. *(United States Navy)*

Radiation is also the most important mechanism of heat transfer in space. Above Earth's atmosphere there is no air and therefore no convection currents. There are also not many bodies available to conduct heat. Astronauts must take into account the physics of heat transfer because they can get into serious trouble simply by floating in sunlight. With no air currents to carry away the heat absorbed from the Sun, astronauts can become dangerously overheated. Shade is essential, as well as cooling mechanisms attached to spacesuits.

But on Earth, all three mechanisms operate freely, which is why designing a thermos bottle requires a considerable amount of skill. Thermos bottles reduce conduction and convection by surrounding the beverage as much as possible with a vacuum (just like in space). The inner and outer surfaces of the thermos (enclosing the vacuum) are covered with a shiny metallic material that reflects more radiation than it absorbs. Although this does not permanently defeat heat transfer, it slows the process considerably. The application of a little bit of physics can keep heat transfer from quickly turning a thermos of chilled milk into a bottle of warm, spoiled sludge.

Cooling Down and Heating Up

Heat transfer has noticeable consequences—changes in temperature. A hot beverage such as coffee gets cool when left on the kitchen table. Frozen vegetables thaw when taken out of the freezer, and they get hot when placed in a pot of boiling water. Temperatures change, and these changes seem to happen in a specific way. Objects gradually become the same temperature as their surroundings.

When two objects at different temperatures come into contact, the warmer object cools down, and the colder object warms up. Heat flows from hot bodies to cold ones and continues to flow until the objects reach the same temperature, which will be somewhere between the two initial temperatures. This is *thermal equilibrium.* For example, a marble at 65°F (18.3°C) and a small steel ball at 75°F (23.9°C) placed together might both end up at a temperature of 68°F (20°C), which is the thermal equilibrium temperature. The heat transfers in this case by conduction—the contact allows the atomic and molecular motion of one object to influence the other. A further change may take place, as the marble and steel gradually adopt the temperature of the surroundings (for instance, the room that holds the objects). After that, there is no change, unless the room temperature changes.

The simple observation that heat flows from hot to cold until objects reach a common temperature is sometimes called the *zeroth law of thermodynamics.* (Zeroth because it is considered to be the most fundamental of thermodynamic laws, but since this law was formulated only after the *first law of thermodynamics* had already been discovered and named, physicists decided to assign it a number even lower than one.)

Another important observation is that the thermal equilibrium temperature is not generally the average of the initial temperatures. In the earlier example, the thermal equilibrium temperature of the marble and steel was not midway between their starting temperatures. Sometimes this can be due to a difference in size, but even if the two objects are the same size, they do not usually cool off or warm up an equal number of degrees as they reach thermal equilibrium. It takes a specific quantity of heat to change the temperature of an object one degree, and that quantity is different for different materials. This is called *heat capacity*. The nature of a material as well as its state have effects on heat flow and temperature, as discussed in the sidebar "Latent Heats and Heat Capacity."

Water has one of the highest heat capacities of any substance. More heat is required to raise the temperature of water by a certain number of degrees than for most other substances. This property of water has a tremendous impact on the world, affecting sea breezes, storms, and other climate and weather features.

Sea breezes are the result of unequal heat capacities of land and water. When the Sun comes out during the day, it warms both the ground and the ocean, but because water absorbs a lot of heat without increasing much in temperature, the ground warms much faster. As the ground gets warm, so does the air above it. Warm air is less dense and so it rises, and the rising air creates an area of low pressure over the land. The pressure of air over the water is higher since this air is cooler, and the high-pressure air moves toward the land. The result is a nice, cool breeze coming from the ocean, enjoyed by the coastal communities in warm climates such as Florida in the United States. At night the situation is reversed, because land becomes cooler than the ocean; shore breezes at night tend to be from land to sea.

Because of their large heat capacity (as well as their large size), oceans hold a huge quantity of thermal energy. This energy has an important connection with the world's weather, and changes in ocean temperature play a role in extremely wide-ranging weather phenomena. A periodic warming of the ocean waters off the South American coast is a critical part of a weather cycle that impacts winds, storms, and temperatures all across Earth. This is called El Niño, part of a weather cycle known as the Southern Oscillation.

Other properties of water are also influential. As discussed in the sidebar "Latent Heats and Heat Capacity," changes in the

Latent Heats and Heat Capacity

The amount of heat required to raise an object's temperature a given number of degrees depends on both the size of the object and its composition. This amount of heat is proportional to mass; for example, twice as much heat is required for an object with twice as much mass. Composition is also important because specific materials have specific heat capacities. To raise the temperature of a small mass of water by one degree requires five times as much heat as the same mass of a metal such as aluminum. Different heat capacities result from the different configurations and types of bonds of a material's components.

Latent heat is energy that exists because of the *state*, or *phase*, of a substance. The state of a material can be a gas, liquid, or solid. Phase transitions—changes in the phase of a material—store or release energy. For example, to turn liquid water into water vapor—to boil it, in other words—requires heat. The heat input does not increase the temperature of boiling water because the temperature stays constant during the phase change (212°F [100°C] at sea level). Instead of making the water molecules move faster (which would increase the temperature), heat coming into the water at the boiling temperature breaks the bonds that make the water molecules stick together, so they fly off in a gaseous state. In the opposite case, this latent heat energy is released when the water molecules get back together (condense) to form a liquid.

The figure illustrates the phase transition between ice and water. Melting an ice cube requires heat from some source, such

phase of a substance require energy, just as raising its temperature does. To melt ice, enough heat must be absorbed to break apart the chemical bonds holding the water molecules together. Heat normally raises the temperature of a substance by causing more atomic and molecular motion, but at certain temperatures, this motion becomes high enough to change the phase of the material—from solid to liquid or liquid to gas. The temperature of boiling water is a constant 212°F (100°C), and the temperature of melting ice is 32°F (0°C); both stay at that temperature during the phase transition, until all the material is changed and heat can again start to change the temperature.

as a candle, a warm room, or the palm of a hand. The reverse transition, when water turns to ice, liberates the same amount of energy into the environment.

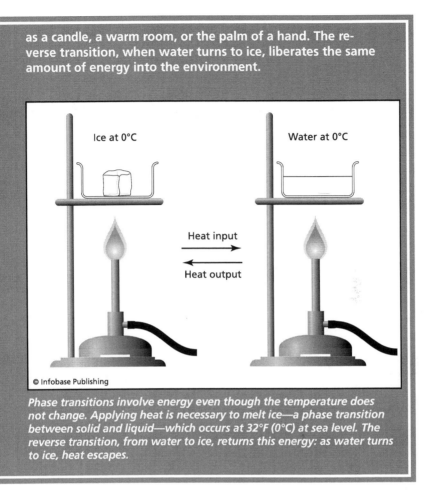

Ice at 0°C

Water at 0°C

Heat input

Heat output

© Infobase Publishing

Phase transitions involve energy even though the temperature does not change. Applying heat is necessary to melt ice—a phase transition between solid and liquid—which occurs at 32°F (0°C) at sea level. The reverse transition, from water to ice, returns this energy: as water turns to ice, heat escapes.

The world would be a different place if this did not occur. After a blizzard, the snow does not disappear all at once but instead absorbs a large quantity of heat as it melts. If this did not happen, all the snow would melt at the same time and cause severe flooding in poor drainage areas. Cities in climates where the temperature fluctuates over and under freezing many times during the winter would suffer a lot of water damage.

Icebergs are big chunks of ice that break off from large ice packs in the polar regions and elsewhere and float around in the ocean. A huge amount of heat must be absorbed from the water to melt them, so they can travel for great distances before disappearing.

The passenger ship RMS *Titanic* met with disaster, costing many lives, when it struck an iceberg in the north Atlantic Ocean on April 14, 1912.

Another interesting property of water causes ice to float in the first place, and this property is related to temperature. Ice is less dense because water expands as it freezes, and so ice floats in water. This is an unusual property. As mentioned earlier, virtually all substances expand when heated. Thermal expansion also occurs for water at temperatures greater than about 39°F (4°C), which is just above freezing. But water contracts when going from 32°F to 39°F (0°C to 4°C). In other words, applying heat to water at 32°F causes it to shrink until it reaches 39°F. This means that water at 39°F is denser than water at any other temperature. As a result, lakes freeze first at the top and do not often freeze all the way to the bottom (unless they are shallow). The reason is because water that gets cooler than 39°F becomes less dense and rises before it reaches the freezing point. Water at the bottom of a freezing pond or lake usually stays about 39°F, a temperature that is above freezing. This is essential for aquatic life to survive the winter; if ponds and lakes froze all the way to the bottom, then all the wildlife in them would die.

Most substances do not have this unusual thermal property. But even the normal kind of thermal expansion can have interesting effects. Although most materials do not expand by a large amount, the forces produced by thermal expansion can be enormous. The force can break glass if it is unevenly heated, causing one part to expand and the other to stay the same. (Since glass is not a good conductor of heat, some time is needed for the temperature to become uniform).

Because concrete and steel also expand when heated, people who build roads, bridges, and other structures must take into account the physics of thermodynamics. A steel beam of length 328 feet (100 m) expands by about 1.9 inches (4.8 cm) if its temperature increases 104°F (40°C)—not a great amount, but since steel is so strong, the beam will push whatever is in its way with an enormous force. If there is no room anywhere in the structure, something has to break.

Engineers often allow for thermal expansion by designing the structure to consist of many small pieces, put together with a slight gap or expansion joint. For example, rubber between two pieces of steel will absorb some of the expansion as the steel becomes hot, and then rebound and maintain the integrity of the structure as the steel cools and shrinks. Expansion joints on bridges are a particular problem because traffic tends to damage them over time, so they need frequent maintenance.

Expansion joints are also a problem on railroads. If a rail was one long piece it would tend to warp as it expanded and might cause a train derailment. Many rails are therefore composed of small pieces with a gap in between to act as an expansion joint. As the train travels down the tracks, the wheels make a click-clack sound as they hit these gaps.

Aside from the sound, the track gaps become intolerable at higher speeds. Passenger trains in parts of Europe travel at hundreds of miles per hour, and jointed track would be bumpy for these high-speed riders. Tracks are instead made of long, continuous stretches of rail. To avoid the warping problem, the builders stretch the rail by applying a great deal of tension. In order to hold the stretched rail in place, strong cross-ties are used, made of concrete instead of wood (as is often used for jointed track). Because the rail is already stretched, it experiences little additional expansion in the normal range of temperatures. An exceptionally hot day can still cause a few problems, but the procedure works quite well. Trains and railroads are old but still useful technologies, relying on powerful locomotives, a large quantity steel, and—just as importantly—a lot of thermodynamics.

Seasons of the Year

Light from the Sun provides energy for Earth and keeps it warm. This is an example of heat transfer by radiation. There are a few sources of heat within Earth itself, but they are small, so without the Sun, the planet would cool off to a temperature too chilly to support life.

But most places on Earth experience changes in the average temperature over the course of a year—changes known as seasons. In the

United States, Canada, Europe, and other places in the Northern Hemisphere, the weather is generally cold in January and warm in July. But the Sun's output of radiation does not change much during the year, so this cannot explain why seasonal changes occur.

One possible explanation for summer's warmth would be if Earth is closer to the Sun in July than January. Because Earth's orbit around the Sun is elliptical rather than circular, the distance from Earth to Sun varies during a complete revolution (one year). But this also cannot be the reason why seasons exist, since Earth is actually farther from the Sun in July than January.

Another reason that the Earth-Sun distance cannot explain the seasons is that the seasons are reversed in the Southern Hemisphere. Australia and other places in the Southern Hemisphere are generally warm in January and cold in July. If distance was the main factor, the seasons would be the same all over the planet.

The real reason for the seasons is that heat transfer by radiation is strongly affected by the angle of incidence, as illustrated by the

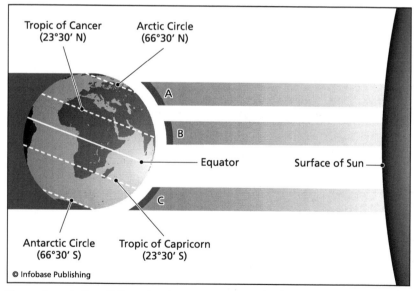

The regions A, B, and C receive the same amount of solar radiation, but in A and C, the radiation is not direct and spreads out over a larger area—these two beams cover a much larger portion of the surface. The energy per unit area in A and C is therefore less than in B.

figure showing the Sun's rays reaching Earth's surface. The angle of incidence is the angle with which radiation strikes the surface. Radiation that strikes an object's surface at a 90-degree angle—perpendicular, or head-on—warms it up much more than when it strikes the object at a lesser angle. At small angles, the energy is more spread out, so there is less energy per unit area than there would be if the radiation struck the surface head-on.

The Sun's radiation does not strike Earth's surface head-on in most places, since the planet is a sphere. Earth's rotational axis is also not oriented perpendicular with respect to its orbital plane, which has important effects as well. The rotational axis is the line passing through Earth's poles, around which it rotates. The orbital plane is a plane drawn through the Sun and Earth. If Earth's rotational axis made a 90-degree angle with this plane—if it were perpendicular to the plane, in other words—then the angle of the Sun's radiation for any given place on Earth would be constant over the course of the year. This is because the planet would be oriented in the same way throughout its orbit as it moves around the Sun.

But Earth's axis is not perpendicular to the orbital plane—it makes an angle of about 23.5 degrees with respect to the perpendicular. The axis, in other words, is tilted. What this means is that for one-half of Earth's orbit about the Sun—which means for one-half of the year—one hemisphere of the globe is tilted toward the Sun, and the other hemisphere is tilted away. The hemisphere that is pointed toward the Sun receives radiation in a more direct manner—the rays strike the surface at an angle close to perpendicular, so this hemisphere receives more energy per area than the other hemisphere. During the months of June and July, the Northern Hemisphere is pointed toward the Sun and the Southern Hemisphere away. The opposite occurs during December and January. The figure on page 22 illustrates these two situations.

The tilt also means that the Sun appears to climb to different heights during the year. The Sun is high in the sky at noon during the summer and low during the winter. Therefore, the days are longer in the summer than the winter (which also plays a role in the warmer weather), and the rays have to pass through less of Earth's atmosphere.

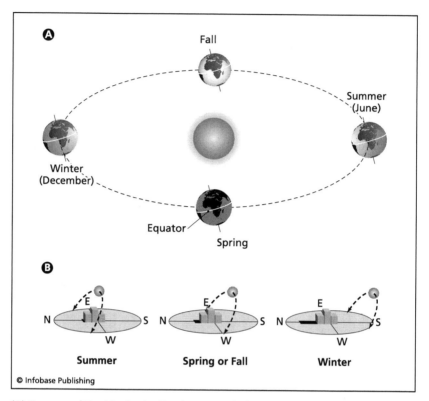

(A) Because of Earth's tilt, the Northern Hemisphere (upper half of the globe in the diagram) receives solar radiation at an angle that is much closer to perpendicular in June than in December. This means that to an observer on Earth, the Sun's path across the sky is much higher in summer than spring, autumn, and especially winter, as illustrated in (B).

The radiation angle has many other effects. Surfaces that face the sunlight, such as the sloping roof of a house, lose their snow coating after a blizzard sooner than surfaces that do not face sunlight. Snow in V-shaped valley walls in the mountains can sometimes last well until spring, because the radiation strikes at an angle far from perpendicular. Snow on roofs can get heavy enough to damage the structure, particularly in places such as Moscow, Russia, that receive a lot of snow during the winter. Getting the snow to melt as fast as possible is an important consideration in the design of buildings in these parts of the world.

Melting snow is not the only aspect of the physics of thermo-dynamics that architects and engineers must keep in mind. Thermodynamics plays an active role in any city's environment.

Urban Heat Islands

Much is different in big cities compared to small towns and farms. The air is more polluted, for example. Cities are also 1–10°F (0.55–5.5°C) warmer than the surrounding area. Weather in a large city can be different than the surrounding area in quite a few ways, and cities have their own distinct weather characteristics—a climate all their own. The reasons have a lot to do with physics, particularly heat transfer and the thermal properties of materials.

The word *urban* comes from a Latin word, *urbs*, meaning city and identifies areas that have a large population and a concentration of buildings and other human-made structures. The regions immediately surrounding the city are known as suburbs, and regions further removed—out in the country with a low population density—are called rural. The discovery that the climate of a city (and often its closest suburbs) differs in significant ways from that of rural areas was made nearly two centuries ago. In the early 1800s, scientist Luke Howard made temperature measurements in London and at short distances away and found that London was warmer by about 1.5°F (0.83°C).

The temperature difference between cities and their surrounding countryside has apparently been increasing, especially in the last few decades. Cities are warming up, much more than rural areas. One study determined that the temperature difference is three times greater than it was 40 years ago.

One reason that cities are warmer than surrounding areas can be guessed by anyone who, on a sunny day, has tried to walk barefoot across asphalt—a blacktop parking lot or street, for example. The surfaces of buildings and roads that are exposed to sunlight can be 50–70°F (27.7–38.9°C) hotter than the air around them. These materials tend to absorb a lot of energy from the Sun, instead of reflecting it away. All materials reflect at least some of the light that hits them (if they did not, they could not be seen,

Even the beautiful city of Honolulu, Hawaii, surrounded by ocean on one side and mountains on the other, is made of construction materials that retain too much heat. *(Kyle Kirkland)*

because unless objects emit light themselves they can only be seen by the light that is reflected from them), but construction materials of urban areas usually reflect less than rural woods and fields. Scientists say that they have low *albedo*.

Heat transfer by radiation occurs by absorption. Because of the energy absorbed by materials commonly used in construction, urban structures get hot. They also tend to stay hot. They start to cool during the evening and at night, but only slowly. This slow rate of cooling is probably why the temperature difference between a city and its surrounding area is even greater during night, generally reaching a maximum around midnight.

Cities are sometimes called urban heat islands because of their warmer temperatures. Heavily populated cities that are spread out over a large area, such as Los Angeles, California, and Tokyo, Japan, are particularly susceptible. Los Angeles is home to about 4 million people and experienced a rapid expansion in the early and middle part of the 20th century as the movie and entertainment industry began to grow. Since the 1940s, the average temperature in Los Angeles has increased about 1°F (0.6°C) every 10 years.

Tokyo is also getting hotter, and in the sweltering summer of 2004, the temperature soared to 109°F (42.8°C).

There are several other factors besides construction materials that make cities hotter. A lot of heat is produced by various machines and factories in the city. Aerosols and particles that commonly exist in urban air may trap the heat. The geometry of cities—the canyons created by the tall buildings—may also play a role. Tokyo, for example, used to receive a sea breeze from the bay that kept the temperatures cool, but now tall buildings block this flow of air.

One of the effects of urban heating is that air around the city gets warmer and rises. The rising air cools and condenses. As a result, clouds form, and sometimes it rains. Cities tend to be about 10 percent more cloudy than the surrounding area and have about an equally higher amount of precipitation. Meteorologists have also observed increased rainfall during the summer months in downwind areas of large cities.

Although the increased temperature is nice in the winter, it does not make up for the problems in the summer. Air conditioners must run longer, which is expensive and produces more air pollution, worsening the situation. Scientists have used satellites and infrared cameras on airplanes to study urban landscapes and have found, for example, that about 56 percent of Sacramento, California, is covered by roofs and pavements, many of which have low albedo and absorb a lot of heat.

What can be done about this? There are several possible ways to reduce the urban heat island effect. Cities could plant more trees and other vegetation, which provide shade and do not get as hot as concrete and asphalt—another reason why parks should be welcome in urban areas. A study in Singapore found that rooftop gardens reduce the temperature at the top of the building by 7°F (3.9°C). Cities could also use construction materials that have a higher reflectivity. Such materials are already available, but they tend to be more costly, so builders often use cheaper materials. Parks are also expensive, at least in an economic sense, because they take up space that could be used for commercial development, which would bring in more revenue for the city.

But the expense would be worthwhile in the long run. The urban climate forms an environment of increasing interest to physicists and meteorologists and is the focus of much scientific research, but one of the most important jobs is getting urban engineers and planners to understand how much of an impact physics has on their climate.

Global Warming

Cities are not the only places getting warmer these days. There has been a lot of discussion recently about a general warming of the Earth: the average temperature at the Earth's surface has increased about 1°F (0.55°C) in the last 100 years. Although the recording of precise temperature measurements only began in the 1860s, scientists who study Earth's past believe that the 20th century was the warmest century in 1,000 years. And since 1861, all of the top-10 warmest years have occurred after 1990. This worldwide effect is called global warming.

One degree in 100 years may not sound like much. But Earth's environment maintains a delicate balance, and serious disruptions can be caused by small changes. This is known as the "butterfly effect," where complex systems such as weather can be affected by seemingly insignificant changes.

If global warming continues, there could be drastic consequences in the not too distant future. Polar ice may melt, causing a rise in sea levels and coastal flooding. The average level of the oceans has already increased about five inches (12.5 cm) in the last 100 years, due in part to land-based glacier melting. (Another reason for the rise could be due to thermal expansion.) Greenland, a continent in the north Atlantic Ocean containing a lot of glacial ice, is closer to the equator, and its glaciers would probably melt before the polar glaciers. If all of Greenland's glaciers melted into the ocean, the average sea level would increase 10–20 feet (3–6 m), which is enough to cause major flooding of coastal areas and low-lying islands. Other disastrous consequences of global warming include an increase in the frequency of severe storms such as hurricanes. The weather may become more variable in general, leading to economic and agricultural difficulties.

An understanding of the reasons for global warming is essential, and physics plays a critical role. But there is an unfortunate problem: the causes of global warming are not easy to grasp and are not fully understood.

As mentioned earlier, cities appear to be getting warmer, but this is not quite the same thing as global warming. In terms of surface area, only a small percentage of the world is urban. And yet, because the planet is becoming increasingly urbanized, some meteorologists believe that urban heating is nevertheless making a contribution to global warming. As cities grow and expand, this contribution will only get bigger.

But many scientists believe that the main source of global warming is the increase in certain gases in Earth's atmosphere. These gases are responsible for the so-called *greenhouse effect*. The greenhouse effect is named after plant nurseries—hence the term *greenhouse*—which are warmed by this process. In greenhouses,

Greenhouses provide warm, comfortable environments for animals and plants. *(Elizabeth Kirkland)*

the heat is trapped not by gases but by glass. Glass allows a wide range of electromagnetic radiation to pass through it, including visible light (glass is transparent), but one type of radiation that does not easily pass through glass is infrared radiation. This is the type of radiation that warm objects tend to emit. Objects inside a greenhouse absorb the Sun's rays, and this energy causes them to get warm. As they get warm, they radiate more infrared, which would normally transfer heat to the surrounding area. But the glass of the greenhouse blocks heat transfer, so the inside is warm even on a cold day.

The same thing happens to the interior of a car on a sunny day, which is why pets and children should never be left inside a closed car. People often leave windows cracked open to keep the inside from becoming so hot. This is a wise decision based on physics—not only does some infrared radiation escape, convection currents carry away some of the heat from the car's interior as well.

If the region surrounding an object permits energy from the Sun's rays to enter but prevents the object from radiating this energy away, the object, such as a greenhouse, will get hot. Earth's atmosphere also does this. The gases of the atmosphere are therefore responsible for a greenhouse effect that warms the surface of the planet. But this is not necessarily bad—the warming due to Earth's atmosphere is essential for life because otherwise the planet would be much cooler. The radiation absorbed from the Sun would be emitted into space as infrared radiation, and in the absence of an atmosphere, Earth would maintain a thermal equilibrium temperature much lower than it is today and probably be too cold for humans to live.

The importance of an atmosphere—or lack thereof—is clear from the study of the planets of the solar system. Mars is so cold, not just because of its greater distance, but because it does not have much of an atmosphere. In the opposite extreme, Venus has an atmosphere 90 times denser than Earth, and its surface temperature is about 860°F (460°C). The effects of an atmosphere can also be clearly demonstrated by observing Mercury, a planet near the Sun that does not have an atmosphere. This is the closest planet to the Sun, but its surface temperature varies greatly. As Mercury rotates (which it does much more slowly than Earth), the side facing the Sun gets exceptionally hot because it absorbs a lot of the Sun's energy, reaching 860°F (460°C). But the other side (the "night" side) is very cold, dropping to about –292°F (–180°C) since the absorbed heat escapes by radiating into space. An atmosphere would cause the day and night temperature difference on Mercury to be far less extreme.

Some atmospheric gases are more effective than others at absorbing infrared radiation. Gases such as carbon dioxide, water vapor, and methane absorb a lot of infrared. These gases exist naturally in the atmosphere, but they can also be generated by human activities—particularly carbon dioxide, which is a product of a lot of economic and technological activity such as the burning of gas and oil. Other chemicals produced by industrial processes, such as hydrofluorocarbons and perfluorocarbons, are even stronger greenhouse gases.

The difficulty in understanding the physics of global warming lies in determining exactly what is causing the warming and how it will affect the future climate. An increase in greenhouse gases can and will contribute to a rise in temperature, but no one is certain how much of the observed global warming has been caused by this effect. Earth has experienced ice ages and warming trends throughout its history, long before human civilization developed. Pinpointing the cause or causes of global warming and its consequences are not easy because of its worldwide scale—scientists cannot reproduce and study these issues in the rigorous, controlled conditions of their laboratories. Instead, understanding and predicting the future course of global warming relies on complicated models and theories, which may or may not be accurate.

The extent of the threat of global warming to the world and civilization is not yet clear. But considering the potential for devastation, it is a problem involving thermodynamics and physical chemistry that demands attention. The study of heat, far from

Apollo 17 astronauts snapped this photograph of Earth on December 7, 1972, as they traveled toward the Moon. *(NASA)*

being simply a curious exercise for physicists, will ultimately prove to have very great effects for Earth—and on a global level, affecting each and every person on the planet.

2

HEAT AND BODY TEMPERATURE

THERMODYNAMICS IS IMPORTANT for the environment, and it is also critical to life. Earth's atmosphere keeps the planet's surface warm, as discussed in the previous chapter, and warmth is closely associated with life. Coldness is associated with death.

But the relation between heat—in terms of a physicist's description of energy flow—and living beings is complex. Life requires an abundance of chemical reactions, as plants and animals use energy to make important molecules responsible for maintaining and repairing tissues. Many of these reactions depend on one another, as the molecules produced in one reaction become participants in the next. Biological tissues must maintain a delicate balance in these reactions, governing their rate so that everything proceeds smoothly. Since temperature affects the rate of chemical reactions, temperature must be regulated as well. Temperature also affects the function of biological molecules, and they cannot do their job if they are too cold or too warm—this is another reason temperature is critical.

Different organisms have different methods of maintaining proper temperature. Studying the temperature of living beings has given biologists insight into the form and function of life and provided an important means of determining the state of health. Doctors and nurses are familiar with the procedure, and one of the first steps in examining a patient involves a thermometer to measure the patient's *body temperature.*

Body Temperature

The human body maintains a relatively constant temperature of about 98.2°F (36.8°C). This temperature fluctuates during the course of day because of natural biological rhythms and other influences, such as the level of activity, but unless a person is sick, the body's temperature stays within a degree or so of normal. The normal temperature is not quite the same for all people, and although this temperature is often given as 98.6°F (37°C)—a number determined in the 19th century from a sample of thousands of patients—more recent measurements show that many people, particularly older adults, have a slightly lower average temperature.

Temperature is a measure of the motion of atoms and molecules, and this motion influences the speed at which most chemical reactions proceed. A chemical reaction usually involves the interaction of two or more molecules, which often must meet or come together in order for the reaction to occur. Higher temperatures mean greater motion, which favors chemical reactions because it brings atoms and molecules together more often. Chemistry is crucial to all living organisms, because life involves a tremendous number of chemical reactions: breaking down food molecules, maintaining and repairing tissue, signaling and communication among cells, and many others.

Another reason body temperature is strictly maintained involves the nature of *proteins.* Proteins are large molecules that perform many different functions in the body. In most cases, a protein must assume a certain shape or form before it can function properly. But at high temperatures, proteins begin to lose their shape—they "unfold" because their constituent atoms and molecules are jiggling around too much to stay in place. This is similar to the melting of ice; by analogy, it can be said that at high temperatures proteins "melt" into a different state, and in this state, they are unable to do their job.

The zeroth law of thermodynamics says that thermal equilibrium should eventually be reached between objects that are able to transfer heat by conduction, convection, or radiation. Room temperature is usually around 68–75°F (20–23.9°C), and the air temperature outside varies but is not often much warmer than 90°F (32.2°C). Human beings are able to maintain a body temperature higher than that, which requires a heat source—otherwise the human body would fall to the temperature of its environment. This heat source will be discussed in a later section.

But the whole body need not be maintained at "body temperature." A person's body temperature generally refers to the core temperature, the temperature inside the body. The skin temperature is usually about 10°F (5.5°C) less than 98.2°F (36.8°C) and on cool days can get much colder. The reason has to do with thermodynamics. Since at least a small portion of skin is almost always exposed to air, the important heat transfer mechanism of convection is operating on it (along with radiation, and possibly also some conduction). Some heat loss from the skin naturally occurs. This is not disastrous, as the skin need not be maintained at 98.2°F in order to function. If the skin had to be 98.2°F, this would be costly in terms of the body's heat supply, considering the constant losses from convection and radiation. The skin and the fat underneath act like a layer of insulation, trapping the heat of the interior, but they do not need to be as warm as the internal organs.

The relative warmth of the body's core temperature means that people can warm their hands by blowing on them with air expelled from the mouth. But this only works when the mouth is held open widely. Air blown from compressed lips expands and loses heat rapidly, so it feels cool.

Since the skin is normally cooler than the interior of the body, nurses and physicians must be careful when they measure a patient's temperature. The important temperature is the core body temperature, not the skin temperature. Health-care providers place the thermometer in the patient's mouth or in other locations that are not continuously exposed to air and room temperature.

Devices other than thermometers can detect the body's warmth. Thermal imagers can see warm objects, such as people, by the amount of emitted infrared radiation. Sensitive imagers can detect the presence of people even if they are concealed by cooler objects, such as behind walls or underneath a pile of rubble. The imagers benefit rescuers by helping them find survivors at night or in collapsed buildings and mining disasters.

Although the body makes every effort to maintain its temperature within a narrow range, occasionally it fails to do so. Because temperature is so important, it does not take a change of many degrees to have a severe, even life-threatening impact.

A drop in body temperature is called *hypothermia* (*hypo* means under or less). Hypothermia does not often occur in people who are adequately bundled up, unless they are outside in winter for long periods of time. But the polar regions are so cold that survival becomes a challenge, as the temperature can drop to –70°F (–56.7°C) or lower. (The record low is –126°F, or approximately –87.8°C.)

Hypothermia is also a big problem for people who become immersed for a period of time in cold water. Water has a high heat capacity, which means it can act like a heat "sponge." A person floating in a cold ocean will become chilled very quickly as the body rapidly loses heat to the water. In cold water such as the north Atlantic Ocean, which is often only a few degrees above freezing, unprotected shipwreck survivors cannot last more than a few hours. The RMS *Titanic* disaster claimed a lot of lives in this way.

At the other extreme, higher temperatures (or hyperthermia) are not welcome either. Unlike hypothermia, however, high temperatures in the form of *fevers* occur quite often.

Fevers are typically part of the body's way of fighting an infection, which is caused by the invasion of some sort of microorganism. Certain substances flowing in the bloodstream produce a fever by their activity on a small part of the brain called the hypothalamus. The hypothalamus is important in many physiological processes, including the regulation of body temperature. During a fever, the hypothalamus causes the body's core temperature to gain a few degrees.

Although a fever is uncomfortable, it seems to serve a purpose—it is the body's attempt to create a less hospitable environment for the invading microorganism. A fever is also associated with increased activity of the immune system, the body's main defense against invaders. But a fever of more than a few degrees above normal can be dangerous. High fevers can produce abnormal brain activity called seizures; one of the reasons these seizures occur is because the high temperature stimulates the chemical reactions in the brain to reach a rate that is too great for proper functioning.

Another type of unusually high body temperature is heatstroke. Heatstroke is particularly dangerous because it is a result of high temperatures that the body cannot control, such as becoming overheated from strenuous activity or being trapped in a hot area. Small children or pets stuck in a car with rolled-up windows on a sunny day will quickly overheat, because the car's "greenhouse effect" sends the temperature inside the car soaring.

How People Sense Hot and Cold

According to the zeroth law of thermodynamics, objects with different temperatures will eventually reach thermal equilibrium if there is a way heat can flow between them. But the zeroth law says nothing about how fast this will occur.

Heat transfer has many options: all objects radiate, convection currents are common, and all objects also conduct heat, at least to a certain extent. But as discussed in the sidebar, some objects are better heat conductors than others, which is important for a lot of reasons, not the least of which is that it affects whether an object is sensed as cool or warm when a person touches it.

A tile floor of the bathroom and a carpet in the bedroom may be at the same temperature—which, in general, would be the room temperature—but they do not feel the same. On a chilly morning, walking across the bathroom's tile floor with bare feet elicits a much colder sensation than the trip across the carpet of the bedroom.

Objects that are good heat conductors will produce stronger temperature sensations than objects that are not. Metal is one

Heat Conductors and Insulators

Some of the best conductors of heat are metals, but not all metals are equally good heat conductors. Silver and brass are about eight times better than steel. Good insulators—the opposite of conductors—include cork, Styrofoam, fiberglass, and air, which all have roughly the same low heat conductivity. Silver conducts heat about 40,000 times better than Styrofoam.

Metals are excellent electrical conductors because of the presence of a large number of mobile electrons, and this is the same reason that metals conduct heat so well. Electrons are charged particles that circle the nucleus of atoms and may also exist freely, outside of atoms. The bonds that hold metal atoms together allow some of the electrons to roam around, so they can carry an electric current—or they can transfer heat. Heating one end of a metal bar causes the electrons to gain kinetic energy, and they jostle their neighbors, which means heat flows quickly down the length of the bar. Plastic such as Styrofoam does not have many mobile particles, so the increased motion associated with higher temperatures takes a longer time to travel through the material.

Tiles made of silica fiber are also insulators. Space shuttles use this material to protect the vehicles and their occupants from reentry temperatures that can reach 2,500°F (1,370°C).

Thermal tiles cover the underside of the space shuttle Discovery, *protecting it from high temperatures during reentry.* (NASA/Stephen K. Robinson)

of the best heat conductors, and when a piece of metal is hot, it feels hot. When touched, heat from the metal flows into skin by conduction, causing an immediate sensation (and the immediate drawing away of the hand or fingers). The opposite case also holds true: when a metal is cold, it feels cold, for heat is conducted rapidly from the skin when a person comes into contact with it. Objects that are not good heat conductors—heat insulators, in other words—do not induce a strong sensation of temperature when they are touched briefly. If contact is maintained, then even insulators will eventually feel warm or cold (if they really are) because thermal equilibrium will always be reached, but this takes some time in the case of insulators.

Devices such as thermometers are often good conductors, and thermal equilibrium is reached quickly. Thermometers reach thermal equilibrium quickly so that they report the correct temperature as soon as possible. The human body has mechanisms that detect temperature as well—this is how people feel hot and cold sensations. But the body's thermometers are much different than an analog or digital thermometer.

Throughout the skin are small nerve endings called receptors. Although scientists do not know as much as they would like about them, it appears that there are different types of receptors for hot temperatures and cold temperatures. The receptors send signals to the brain, which interprets these signals as "hot" or "cold" depending on which receptors are doing the signaling and the strength of the signal. When people sense temperature, they are generally not sensing the temperature of the air or the object they are touching but instead the temperature of the skin in which the sensors are embedded.

A good thermometer always indicates the same number of degrees for the same temperature, but human sensations of hot and cold do not. People's thermal sense is relative. If a person puts one hand in cold water and the other hand in warm water, waits a while, then quickly puts both hands in the same bucket of tepid water (neither warm nor cold), the two hands have different sensations. To one hand, the tepid water feels warm, but to the other, it feels cold. The human sense of temperature depends on what the person has experienced immediately before. To the hand that has been in cold water, the tepid water feels warm; to the hand that has been in warm water, the same tepid water feels cool.

Adaptation of the body's "thermometers" means that if people experience a warm or cool environment for a long time, gradually the awareness of the temperature decreases. This is adaptation—people no longer feel the warmth or coolness until there is a change in temperature. Adaptation also occurs in other senses of the body, such as touch; a person feels a wristwatch when it is first put on, but later the wearer hardly notices the wristwatch unless attention is for some reason drawn to it.

The human sense of temperature detects not only hot and cold but also certain chemicals. These chemicals activate the temperature receptors, causing a sensation of hot or cold. This is what happens when a person eats "hot" foods such as chili peppers. The food itself need not be hot (though sometimes it is). There is a chemical in chili peppers called capsaicin that stimulates hot receptors in the tongue, producing a burning sensation when eating these foods. At the other extreme, a chemical called menthol elicits a cool sensation. This chemical is either a natural component or an added flavoring of many mints.

The human sense of temperature is clearly not the most accurate thermometer, at least to the high standards of scientific measurement. The senses were not meant to provide precise physical measurements, as a physicist desires, but rather to help people survive in the environment. As such, they do their job very well.

Other animals have different receptors. Some snakes, such as rattlesnakes, have infrared receptors located on their face, enabling them to detect heat sources from a distance. They do not need to touch the object and provide a path for heat conduction, for these receptors detect radiation. These snakes are able to hunt prey by sensing the prey's body heat. A warm object against a cool background stands out noticeably to an infrared detector, and there is little that a mouse or other small animal can do to cover up its heat "signature."

Warm-Blooded and Cold-Blooded Animals

People often describe animals as either warm-blooded or cold-blooded, depending on how well or how poorly they can generate body heat. Warm-blooded animals like birds and mammals (including people) can generate and maintain high body temperature. The average body temperature for a healthy person is about 98.2°F (36.8°C); for a healthy cow, the average is around 101.5°F (38.6°C).

Cold-blooded animals like most fish, reptiles, insects, and amphibians are generally unable to regulate their body temperature. Their body temperature varies with the environment—the animals are cold on chilly days, warm on hot ones. The scientific term for the ability to generate internal heat is called *endothermy* (*endo* means inside or internal). Having a temperature that depends mostly on the environment is called *ectothermy* (*ecto* means outside or external).

The physics of body heat is based on energy conversion. The law of energy conservation says that energy may be transformed

This reptile, a caiman, absorbs some of the Sun's radiation. The animal is probably already quite warm, since it does not seem to mind that part of its body is in the shade. *(Elizabeth Kirkland)*

from one form to another but is never lost. Heat is a form of energy, and it is commonly produced in a large number of situations, as noted earlier. Burning logs produce a lot of heat, as the chemical energy of the wood is converted into light as well as thermal energy. The body extracts energy in a similar way, by "burning" foods that are rich in energy, particularly carbohydrates and fats. Unlike the burning of logs, the burning of food is slower and more controlled, but it is essentially a similar process. (The reason people and animals require oxygen is to support this "combustion.") Some of this food energy drives chemical reactions that maintain and repair body tissues, but the body converts some of it—especially in endothermic animals—into heat.

For endothermic animals, the body is like a furnace, burning part of the fuel (supplied as food) to keep warm. Muscular activity will also produce some heat—when cool, people often move around to get "warmed up."

The benefits of endothermy are enormous. Muscles do not work well when cold because the physiological processes that cause them to contract are slow at low temperatures. (This is another example of the general rule that high temperatures speed things up and low temperatures slow things down.) When muscles are warm, they work faster, so the animal can be more active and move around more quickly. Warmed-up muscles mean a better chance of catching prey and avoiding predators. Warm-blooded animals are not restricted by the environment; they can be active at any time of the day or night, even if it is cold. If a warm-blooded animal has sufficient fur or other insulation, it can live almost anywhere—even in the polar regions, as polar bears do.

Cold-blooded animals cannot survive in continually cold weather. They are sluggish in the cold because their bodies (including their muscles) tend to be at the same temperature as their environment. Ectothermic animals will often bask in the sun on chilly days in order to warm their bodies. But they know how to do this effectively because their instincts have developed in accordance with the laws of physics. Ectothermic animals orient their bodies in the most effective manner while basking—they position themselves so that the sunlight strikes their body at an angle as close to perpendicular as possible in order to maximize the energy transfer.

Fish are ectothermic, which raises special problems. Water soaks up a lot of thermal energy, and many types of fish lose a great deal of body heat through the gills. A lot of blood flows through the gills, because this is where it picks up oxygen to circulate to other tissues. Cold water chills the blood rapidly, and the blood consequently chills the animal as it circulates—in other words, it is a convection current.

Yet fish manage to survive because their physiology is adapted to life in water. Some fish even have proteins in their blood that act as antifreeze, preventing the blood from freezing and allowing the fish to survive in cold water. But a lot of species of fish are constrained to live in warm, tropical waters because they cannot endure the cold for very long. Size is important because of simple thermodynamics: a small fish will lose body heat rapidly, since it has a great deal of surface area in contact with the water. A large fish, such as a great white shark, has a lot of bulk, so that even though its surface area is greater than a small fish, a lot of its interior is insulated from the cold water.

But there are some kinds of fish that manage to keep their body temperature relatively warm even in cool water. Tunas and certain types of sharks (called mackerel sharks) are able to maintain a body temperature as high as 20°F (11.1°C) above the water temperature. Tunas have networks built into their blood system to conserve heat that would be lost by the blood when it passes through the gills. Mackerel sharks have special organs that retain some of the heat produced by their muscular activity. Even though these fish are considered "cold-blooded," they are not quite as cold-blooded as most of the other fish swimming around in the ocean.

Although warm-bloodedness is advantageous because it gives an animal some independence from the environment, there is a great cost. Because a considerable portion of the fuel provided by food is burned for warmth, endothermic animals must eat more than ectothermic ones. Much of the extra activity created by warm-bloodedness is spent finding enough food to keep the interior fire lit and burning.

One of the more interesting questions about dinosaurs is whether they were warm-blooded or cold-blooded. In terms of evolution, dinosaurs have ties to both cold-blooded reptiles and warm-blooded birds. But fossils leave little clues as to the thermal nature of dinosaurs. Most scientists are not sure whether dinosaurs were cold- or warm-blooded, although what little evidence is available suggests that at least some dinosaurs were warm-blooded.

It is possible that some dinosaurs were cold-blooded and some were warm-blooded or perhaps possessed characteristics that were a combination of the two. There are a variety of animals existing today that are similar; the tunas and mackerel sharks mentioned above are examples, as are certain bats, which, although mammals, are not able to regulate their body temperature. Although no one knows for certain about dinosaurs in general, the physics of thermodynamics indicates that the larger dinosaurs would have been able to retain a significant portion of their body heat simply due to their size and bulk. This is true even if they had no active "furnace" burning inside.

The Comfort Zone: Maintaining the Right Temperature

Although endothermic animals consume a lot of food in order to burn some of it for warmth, there are other techniques to stay warm in the winter. Thermodynamics provides clues for how best to go about it. There are also ways to stay cool in the summer.

Human beings thrive in a relatively narrow range of temperature. Although people are endothermic animals, the internal temperature regulation is not sufficiently strong to withstand the challenges of continually cold or hot weather without clothes, heaters, air conditioners, and other technological help. Exposure to temperature extremes for even a short period of time, or prolonged exposure to less extreme but abnormal temperatures, can result in severe injury or death of the individual.

Early human beings lived in tropical climates, where it was warm. They could not venture into colder areas of the world because they could not survive. But this changed once people learned to imitate the animals; the earliest clothing worn to keep the human body warm was probably fur. Animal fur offers thermal insulation and retains body heat, so the internal temperature regulation does not get overworked. To do this, fur employs thermodynamic principles and air, an excellent thermal insulator.

Fur insulates by trapping air in the little spaces between the hairs. Body heat warms this air, and since the air cannot go anywhere, it stays next to the skin, so a layer of warm air surrounds the animal. The trapped air loses little heat to the surroundings because air is a poor conductor. Just as important, the trapped air does not escape and become replaced by cold air. This is what happens to the bare skin of animals without fur (including humans): the body warms a thin layer of air covering it, but when the air moves—even a gentle breeze, or perhaps the body moves instead—this warmth is gone, and the body must warm the next layer of air (the cold air that rushes in to replace the warm air). The cycle repeats. Convection currents will always carry away a significant amount of body heat if they are allowed to exist.

Feathers work in a similar way to keep birds from losing heat. Feathers also have other functions, but this is true in many cases in biology. Organs and structures perform more than one job.

Fur or feathers are essential for the survival of many small animals, who spend a great deal of time keeping their fur clean. Mice and other rodents, for example, are habitual fur-cleaners, grooming themselves constantly. Animals living around the water, such as otters and sea birds, also spend much time keeping their fur or feathers clean. The disastrous consequence of failing to do so can be seen in the recent accidents involving oceangoing tanker ships. A coating of oil squeezes the trapped air out of fur; oily fur provides no insulation and also causes some buoyancy problems for animals that float in the water. If the animal cannot get the oil out of its fur, it will die of the cold, but in the attempt to clean the fur by licking it, the animal ingests poisonous compounds from the oil. This is one of the most unfortunate aspects of oil spills from tankers. The *Exxon-Valdez* accident in 1989 killed many thousands of animals.

When worn in layers, clothing performs the same function as fur, since the air trapped among the layers provides insulation. A thin undershirt, covered by a shirt, which is in turn covered by a lightweight jacket, offers excellent thermal insulation. But like fur, there can be problems—wet clothes offer little protection.

Some marine animals also use thick deposits of fat as insulation. Blubber found in whales forms a protective layer, helping retain heat in the internal organs and muscles.

Although insulation of any type aids the retention of body heat, it does not produce heat. If the core body temperature drops too low, the body must somehow generate heat quickly (more quickly than usual). Cold-blooded animals such as lizards will seek sunlight or burrow into the warm soil. A dog or a person might move around and warm themselves up; this works because muscular activity produces heat—exercise raises body temperature to as much as 100°F (37.7°C).

The temperature regulation maintained by most warm-blooded animals does not allow the core body temperature to drop too often. But in harsh environments, such as immersion in cold water, a drop in temperature cannot be avoided. In such cases, some animals, including humans, have an involuntary mechanism called shivering that desperately tries to produce heat as fast as possible.

Shivering is a rapid contraction of muscles. It is involuntary, meaning that a person does not consciously decide to shiver. The thermal regulatory system of the body triggers a bout of shivering; if it detects a drop in core body temperature, even only a few degrees, the nervous system will activate large muscles of the body in the attempt to produce heat. Drops in skin temperature are not as important, so usually only decreases in core body temperature will cause the movement.

Too high a temperature is just as serious. The body cannot tolerate increases in temperature any more than it can tolerate decreases. But humans have more effective adaptations to warm weather than to cold, probably because early humans evolved in tropical climates. The most important means that people and other mammals use to cool off when they get too hot is by sweating.

Sweating is a marvelous thermodynamic technique based on the latent heat of water. The phase transition from liquid water to gaseous water (usually called water vapor) absorbs a lot of energy. As discussed in the earlier sidebar "Latent Heats and Heat Capacity," absorbing heat will cause an object's temperature to rise except when it is making a phase transition, in which case the energy goes to breaking bonds. Sweating is such a good way to cool off because when water is placed on warm skin, it evaporates. As it evaporates, water soaks up energy, in the form of heat, decreasing skin temperature.

Glands near the surface of the skin produce sweat. Water is essential to life, but the body sacrifices some of it in order to produce this critical cooling process. A healthy person can lose water at a rate of up to a gallon per hour over a short period of time, but this cannot be sustained. Over the course of a day, a quart an hour is a more sustainable average. But even at the lower rate, the water must be replenished quickly.

Another way the body cools down is by controlling the flow of blood. If the blood vessels in the skin are wide open, a lot of blood flows in these vessels. This makes the skin look flushed. The blood, being mostly liquid, carries heat away from the warm internal organs and toward the skin, where sweating (and possibly cooler air temperatures) should be able to get rid of some of it.

This mechanism also works in the other direction. When it is cold, the body restricts the flow of blood to the skin. The blood then circulates mostly in the interior, where the temperature is usually much warmer than the skin. The skin looks pale under these conditions because there is little blood near the surface. But there are a few areas of the body in which this does not happen. One of these areas is the scalp, where the blood continues to flow near the skin, even when the skin is cold. A lot of heat can be lost if the head is exposed, and human hair is not a very effective insulator. This is why it is a good idea to wear a hat on cold days.

Wind increases the rate of heat loss—this is convection at work. Weather scientists often give the "windchill factor," which is not the actual temperature of the air but rather takes into account the convection produced by winds. If a wet person is exposed to the wind, this makes the heat loss even greater, thanks to the combination of convection and evaporation.

People make considerable effort to maintain the proper temperature in their environment, whether it is the home or the office. Heaters and air conditioners are obviously of much help. Even before such useful inventions, though, people with a little bit of thermodynamics knowledge could go a long way to keep their habitat comfortable. In cold weather, people lit fires, which provided warmth, although they could also be dangerous—particularly for those who lived in wooden structures.

The big problem was staying cool in the summer. This is why homes used to be built and designed with cooling in mind. Ceilings were high to keep hot roofs as far away from the rooms as possible. Trees provided shade. Windows were placed so that they would provide cross-ventilation. Cool breezes were given every opportunity to arise. Now that the energy to run air conditioners is becoming increasingly expensive and scarce, perhaps it is time to once again pay attention to the principles of thermodynamics while constructing homes and offices.

The high roof of this Mississippi house, along with effective ventilation, helps moderate the temperature inside during hot summer days. *(Elizabeth Kirkland)*

Thermography

Nurses and physicians often need to measure a patient's body temperature, which is essential for diagnosing fevers and helpful in understanding other illnesses as well. Since the core body temperature is the most important, the thermometer goes under the patient's tongue for a minute or two so that thermal equilibrium will occur. The thermometer will then be approximately the same temperature as the patient.

But this procedure, while useful, presents an extremely simple picture of the patient's body temperature. The measurement gives a single number, the reading of the thermometer. But the patient's temperature is not the same throughout the body; as already mentioned, the skin temperature is rarely the same as that of the internal organs. Even the core body temperature is not perfectly uniform. The differences within the core are usually small in magnitude, on the order of a fraction of a degree or so, but they do exist. The differences, small though they may be, can be quite important in determining the patient's state of health.

Thermography is a technique of measuring the distribution of temperature in an object or body. As described in the section "Urban Heat Islands," thermography has been used to examine the temperature distribution of urban areas, identifying specific hot spots. Because hot spots are warmer than the surrounding area, they emit more energy. The opposite is true for cold spots. When the detector converts temperature values into color images—often with "warm" colors such as orange and red representing higher temperatures and "cool" colors such as blue representing lower temperatures—thermography produces a map of hot and cold spots. Although it is possible to make a temperature map with a bunch of thermometers (and a lot of patience), sensitive infrared detectors work faster.

Thermographic measurements give a more complete picture of the temperature of an object or region than a single number can. Another advantage is that a technique based on infrared radiation can be done at a distance, without having to touch the object of interest. In some cases it is not possible to get near enough to the object to use a conduction-based thermometer, and in other cases, when the object is extremely hot or cold, it is undesirable to do so. With infrared detectors, there is also no need to wait for thermal equilibrium between the object and the thermometer.

For some disorders of the human body, thermography yields valuable information. The temperature of diseased tissue is sometimes different than that of the rest of the body, usually due to an abnormal flow of blood in and around the unhealthy tissue. An excess of blood often drives up the temperature of the spot, although the increase is slight.

But thermography is not a perfect tool for detecting diseases. A big problem is that because thermography measures infrared radiation emitted by the object, it can only determine the temperature at or near the surfaces that are exposed to the detector. The heat below the surface is not easily observed in this technique, unless it happens to warm up the surface significantly as well. This limits the effectiveness of thermography because it cannot "see" far into the body.

Yet thermography has proven particularly beneficial to veterinarians, who sometimes use it in the diagnosis of diseases in horses and other animals. Hot or cold spots lead veterinarians to the source of the problem, which is valuable because horses are unable to tell the doctor exactly where it hurts.

Thermography is also useful for detecting situations that could cause a lot of harm to animal habitats. Infrared scans can sometimes trace pollution in streams, rivers, and lakes. Waste liquids from leaking sewers or industrial drain systems are typically warmer than the natural river or lake water, especially in the winter. A thermographic map covering a large area may be able to track a warm trickle containing pollution back to its source. This identifies the offender, who then must take steps to correct the problem. This process is important not only to save water life but also to protect sources of drinking water from contamination.

As sensors improve, thermography will become even more useful. An increased knowledge of temperature variations in an object or system will in a lot of cases lead to a more complete understanding of how it works and what to do when something goes wrong.

Extreme Temperatures and Life

Extremely hot or extremely cold temperatures are not normally compatible with life. There are several reasons for this, including the chemical reactions discussed earlier. But one of the most important reasons of all is that life depends on water.

The human body is about 65 percent water by weight. All forms of life, whether plant or animal, are composed of little compartments called cells, which are surrounded by a membrane made mostly of lipids (fats). The fluid inside and outside of cells is water that contains molecules critical to all of the chemical reactions necessary for life. At boiling or freezing temperatures, these solutions can no longer exist—and neither can life.

Even smaller changes can have a lot of effects; it does not take temperatures as extreme as boiling and freezing points to cause problems. As mentioned earlier, the rate at which chemical reactions proceed depends on temperature—in general, the higher the temperature, the faster the reaction. But plants and animals have many different reactions going on at any given time, with the output of one reaction providing the input of another. These chains of linked reactions must work together, and most life-forms require the reaction rates to be carefully controlled. Temperatures must be relatively constant to do so.

Another important concern involving chemical reactions is the molecules that help them to occur. These molecules are known as *enzymes,* which typically help reactions to occur by bringing together the *reactants.* The reactants are the molecules participating in the reaction, and most of them are free to move around. If they had to meet each other by chance in order to react, the reaction would seldom occur. Enzymes often work by temporarily binding the reactants so that they will encounter each other. Most enzymes are large molecules called proteins. As described in the section "Body Temperature," most proteins have a specific shape or geometric configuration that is critical to their function, and this is certainly true of enzymes. Biologists call this shape the protein's *conformation.* An enzyme, for example, may form pockets where two or more reactants are bound and held until they react. But temperatures even just a few tens of degrees warmer than body temperature cause a protein to lose its conformation because the bonds that form the shape are broken.

Human beings cannot afford to let the body temperature get too high, because vital proteins will stop functioning and chemical reactions will proceed too quickly. On the other hand, chemical reactions will proceed too slowly if the body temperature gets too low. Maintaining the proper temperature within strict limits is essential. All animals, especially small ones such as microorganisms, can be killed by heat or cold. Surgeons sterilize their instruments in order to destroy microorganisms such as bacteria that could invade the body as the surgery proceeds. One way to sterilize an instrument is to put it in boiling water for several minutes.

But scientists made a surprising discovery in the middle of the 20th century. They found tiny microorganisms inhabiting hot springs and other places having temperatures that biologists had formerly assumed could not possibly harbor life.

It turns out that many species of one branch of life, called Archaea, actually exist in extreme environments. They are known as *thermophiles* (the name means heat lovers). These microorganisms eat substances that other animals are not able to metabolize (digest), such as sulfur, hydrogen, and compounds containing these elements. They survive, even thrive, in volcanic vents, acidic hot springs, hot-water vents deep in the ocean, and other inhospitable environments. (They can also thrive in artificial environments such as power plants and hot-water heaters.)

Thermophiles survive in extreme temperatures because their proteins are exceptionally sturdy. Somehow these proteins manage to maintain their shape even when the atoms and molecules are jiggling around violently. The bonds holding together the shape must be extraordinary.

There is a steep price to pay for this amazing ability—thermophiles cannot survive elsewhere. They not only thrive on heat, but they also require it. Surgeons need not worry that their sterilization procedure does not kill these microbes, because they are not likely to invade the patient's body. It is too cold for them to grow!

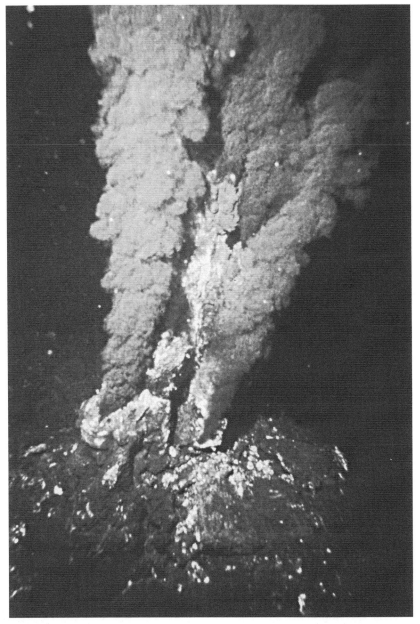

Hydrothermal (hot water) vents like this one on the ocean floor spew out hot, mineral-rich water from beneath Earth's crust. The cold water of the ocean causes some of the minerals to collect and solidify, forming particles that make the emission appear dark in color. *(NOAA/OAR/NURP/P. Rona)*

But these microbes have proven to be important in other ways. A remarkable enzyme from one of these thermophiles is used in laboratories across the globe, in procedures as wide-ranging as medical diagnosis and forensics (analysis of crime scene evidence). Since this enzyme can withstand high temperatures, it can be used in techniques that require molecules to be repeatedly subjected to heating. One technique, called polymerase chain reaction (PCR), replicates DNA molecules so that they can be sequenced and identified. PCR helps in diagnosing genetic diseases as well as identifying blood and hair samples found at crimes scenes.

In the opposite extreme, at frigid temperatures, chemical reactions do not go fast enough to support life. Freezing is also a big concern. But freezing is beneficial as a way to maintain dead tissue from decomposing. It can do this because freezing is so incompatible with life; microorganisms that would otherwise cause decay and decomposition cannot survive. People store certain foods in the freezer—or in the refrigerator, if freezing is not required or desirable—to stop or slow down the activity of bacteria and other microbes.

Freezing has another potential function, to preserve people who have recently died. Called cryonics, the idea is to keep a deceased person's body from decomposing until some unspecified time in the future, when whatever accident or disease that caused the death can be reversed or treated. Because it is so expensive to maintain something as large as body in cold storage, sometimes only the head or brain is preserved. Cryonics is not very popular, but thousands of people have done it.

The unfortunate truth is that cryonics will probably not be successful. The reason is simple and has been noted several times already: water expands when frozen. As a person's tissues freeze, the body's huge amount of water also freezes. Ice forms and grows too big for the delicate membranes that enclose the body's cells, disrupting the membranes. There is little chance that such massive cellular damage can be repaired any time in the near future, and even freezing will not preserve tissue forever. Cryonics consumes a great deal of resources, usually drained from the deceased's estate (which would otherwise go to surviving relatives), and a belief in cryonics requires perhaps too much optimism about future society's charity, economy, and medical technology.

Life has adapted well to thermodynamics, but there are limits to any successful strategy. Although the structure of proteins and the chemistry underlying life may survive at extreme temperatures in special circumstances, most often there is a narrow comfort zone that must be maintained. Whether living beings generate most of their own body heat or get it from the environment, temperature is a concern for all.

3

HEAT AND TECHNOLOGY

M OST PEOPLE USE ice to cool a drink without giving it any thought at all, for ice is easy to make in the freezer compartment of a refrigerator. But not too long ago, ice in the summer was a rare treat. Consumers could purchase frozen water only from a few merchants or businesses that either brought in a large block of ice from a cold climate or had stored some ice during the winter in a dark, cold cellar.

Warming a cold object has always been easy—one need only light a fire. But cooling down a warm object is not so simple. People today are fortunate to have air conditioners, refrigerators, and freezers and are also able to warm up objects in a much more controlled and safe manner than sticking them in a flame or in a pot of boiling water.

Maintaining a relatively constant temperature is important in a huge number of situations. The previous chapter discussed perhaps the most vital one—body temperature. Biological processes require temperatures to be held in a narrow range, and the principles of thermodynamics are critical to living organisms. But a lot of processes in industry, electronics, and elsewhere are sensitive to heat. Temperature regulation in these circumstances also depends on the physics of thermodynamics.

Using Technology to Control Temperature

Keeping the temperature from changing means that one must be prepared to apply heat if the temperature begins to decrease or draw heat away if the temperature begins to increase. Thermodynamics says that heat is energy, and there are definite laws of physics that govern heat and other forms of energy. The sidebar on page 57 discusses one of these laws, called the first law of thermodynamics.

Perhaps the biggest problem in maintaining temperature within a narrow range is that heat is so readily produced by motion. Heat is motion—the motion of atoms and molecules. Friction causes the atoms and molecules of objects to jiggle around with increased vigor, and the result is a rise in temperature.

In general, activity tends to increase temperature. Muscles warm up when people exercise, and this heat must be drawn out of the body in order to maintain the appropriate temperature. This is done in humans by the evaporation of sweat, as discussed in the previous chapter. Electrical machines and devices also need to be cooled down. Heat from electrical currents is evident in certain devices such as electronic heating elements in stoves and ovens. But in cooking implements, heat performs a useful function; in many other situations, heat is not desirable.

Small currents produce only a minor amount of heating, and many of today's electrical equipment get by with a minimum of current. Even so, some heating is inevitable. Electric charges must move to produce a current, and as they rattle around in the electric conductor, they generate heat. Heat is a big problem with computers and other devices that rely on tiny microcircuits etched on silicon wafers, called integrated circuit (IC) chips. Although these tiny circuits use only tiny currents, because the circuits are so small only a little heat will increase their temperature. Due to the nature of the material, ICs stop working if they get too hot. For this reason, modern computers always come equipped with fans, which blow air on the electrical components in danger of overheating. The circulating air creates convection currents to carry away excess heat.

First Law of Thermodynamics

The first law of thermodynamics states that the change in an object's internal energy equals the heat flowing into or out of the object, minus the work the object does on its surroundings. An object loses energy by doing work or because heat flows out of it, and it gains energy if heat flows into it or work is done on the object.

Internal energy is the random motion of the object's molecules (which as mentioned in the first chapter are always moving). All moving objects have energy, called kinetic energy, but people cannot see the motion associated with internal energy since atoms and molecules are so small. Yet this energy exists, even in an object such as a glass of water that is sitting on a table; the water appears to be still since its molecules have no ordered motion—they are not all moving to the left or to the right—but the molecules are moving randomly in different directions, and this motion is energy. As the previous chapters discussed, heat flowing into the object increases this motion, and heat flowing out decreases it.

Work is the result of a force acting over a distance, such as lifting a weight or pushing a cart. Doing work requires a source of energy, which comes from the object doing the work. In physics, the law of energy conservation states that energy is neither created nor destroyed but can be transformed into one form or another. Lifting a weight is work, but the energy required by the process is "stored" in the potential of the lifted weight—when it falls, the weight can do work, as in dams that use falling water to produce electricity. But pushing a cart across a level street is also work, yet the cart does not seem to gain any potential energy—the cart cannot get back on its own or do work in the process.

The first law of thermodynamics accounts for all energy transformations, which include the disordered motion created by friction. In the example of the pushed cart, the tires and the street became a little warmer because they were rubbed together. Energy is conserved, but orderly motion, such as the movement of a cart across a street, can be transformed into disordered motion of the object's molecules—internal energy.

Heat can do work, and *heat engines* are the subject of chapter 4. But there are special circumstances involved in using random internal motion to do work, and the first law of thermodynamics is not the whole story. The second law, discussed below, addresses this issue.

Convection currents are often used for cooling purposes. As one of the mechanisms of heat transfer, these currents are well suited to do so. The circulating air or water draws off heat, and then deposits it elsewhere.

A car radiator works by the circulation of a liquid through pipes and hoses in and around the engine. The liquid is usually water, with antifreeze compounds added so that the liquid does not freeze during the winter. Water, having a large heat capacity, does an excellent job of absorbing heat from the engine. But that heat must be deposited somewhere before the water can come around to the engine again and absorb some more. This is the job of the radiator, which exposes the water to air rushing by (due to the car's motion or, when it is not moving, a fan). This is another convection current, generated by movement of the car through the air. The water is cooled by this "breeze" and returns to the engine to pick up some more heat.

The radiator has a name that sounds like the term *radiation*, which is another mechanism of heat transfer. Although some radiation is always involved in warm objects, the primary job of the car's radiator is to use convection currents to cool down the engine.

Elephants have radiators, in the same sense that cars do. In an elephant, the radiators are their ears. They work because warm blood flows through vessels in an elephant's ears, which are large and thin. The convection current cools down the blood, which then passes through the body again and picks up some more heat. But in cold weather an elephant would prefer to hide its ears, or at least keep them close to its body, in order to conserve heat and maintain body temperature.

Large power plants, which produce much of the country's electricity, also have problems with overheating. Considering the huge electric currents that power plants must generate, this is not surprising. Many power companies use convection currents in the same way as automobile radiators, by circulating cold water.

But there is a problem with this method when it is used by power companies. Power plants, unlike cars, are never traveling down the highway at a high rate of speed. How does the circulating water get rid of its heat? The heat has to go somewhere—the first

This elephant is keeping its ears close to its body to conserve warmth on a chilly day in December. *(Elizabeth Kirkland)*

law of thermodynamics insists upon it. Energy does not simply vanish.

The solution to this problem has unfortunate consequences. Since the water used by power companies does not get rid of its heat, the power company gets rid of the warm water and draws some more cold water from the same source. The source is usually a stream, river, or lake. The circulation of water is therefore not contained within the power plant but consists of the whole water source—the power plant draws off cold water and returns warm water. This process has been described as thermal pollution; in the same way that released chemicals create chemical pollution, released heat creates thermal pollution. Rivers and lakes that experience thermal pollution can suffer adverse effects, especially to their wildlife. The laws of physics are fairly strict about this, and the heat produced by power plants has to go somewhere. But this does not mean that delicate natural environments should be destroyed, and physicists and engineers are working on ways to cool down power generators with as little environmental disruption as possible.

The other two heat transfer mechanisms (conduction and radiation) can also control temperature, but they are not as widely used as convection. Engineers design certain parts of a spaceship to lose excess heat by radiation; this is necessary in the vacuum of space because there are no convection currents. Soldering electronic components involves the application of high temperature, but heat can ruin the component. To prevent this, soldering technicians attach a heat sink to the electronic component. The heat sink is a large piece of metal that conducts away a lot of the heat generated by soldering.

Refrigerators and Air Conditioners

Heat flows from hot to cold. This is the "downhill" path for heat. Just as water naturally flows from a higher elevation to a lower one, heat naturally flows from a hot object to a cold one.

If the inside of a house is warm on a cold winter day, some of the heat escapes to the outside. On a warm summer day, heat flows from outside to inside, making the house uncomfortably hot. The appropriate action for the cold winter day is to light a fire or turn on a heater; in the summer, the occupants switch on the air conditioner.

An air conditioner lowers the temperature of the inside of a room or a house by removing heat. If a very cold object was nearby, the heat could be drawn off by conduction. But in the absence of a conveniently located mountain of ice to absorb the heat, something else must suffice. About 100 years ago, the first air conditioners appeared. In the 1910s and 1920s, movie theaters began to use air conditioners as an added attraction, and for some people, escaping a hot day was the primary reason they went to the movies. Theater billboards proclaimed "It's 20 degrees cooler inside!" Which was true, thanks to air conditioning.

The reason cooling from air conditioners was not available sooner is due to thermodynamics. Heat flows from hot to cold objects, but on a summer day the need is to move heat from inside a building to the outside. This means heat must flow from a relatively cool object to a warmer one. This is against the natural flow of heat, somewhat like pushing heat "uphill." Moving heat uphill requires energy, just as raising water from a lower elevation to a higher one does. The greater the temperature difference between the cool and warm object, the more the air conditioner has to work to push the heat against its natural flow. This work is why air conditioners have power cords—electricity is the energy source.

Since the heat moves from inside to outside, air conditioners need to have access to both the interior and exterior of the house. Air conditioners that cool big buildings have parts distributed both inside and out. Small air conditioners that cool a room are simply placed in a window; one part of the air conditioner faces inside and the other faces outside. The heat must be deposited outside, rather than simply destroyed. It would be easier to just eliminate the heat rather than moving it against its natural flow, but the first law of thermodynamics takes a very dim view of such activity. Heat is energy, and energy cannot be destroyed.

But the first law of thermodynamics allows energy to be transformed. Instead of moving the heat from inside to outside, perhaps it could be transformed into another type of energy. Turning heat into a form of energy such as electricity that can do some sort of useful work would be fantastic. If enough electricity could be generated, it would supply the energy to move the heat "uphill"— this would mean that air conditioners would not require electricity from an outside source, for they could provide all the energy for their needs by conversion of heat. Under these circumstances, air-conditioning would be free—no more bills from the power company.

It would be nice to escape paying the power company for air-conditioning, but here comes another law. As discussed in the sidebar, the *second law of thermodynamics* puts strict limits on the conversion of heat to work. Heat can move around, but people cannot convert all of it into work or into another, more useful form of energy.

Air conditioners have but one option. They must use energy to transport heat from inside to outside. As shown in the figure on page 63, there are three main parts to any air conditioner: evaporator, condenser, and compressor. The evaporator is a long metal tube that puts a circulating fluid, called the working fluid, at low pressure. The fluid enters the evaporator as a warm liquid, but

Second Law of Thermodynamics

The second law of thermodynamics says that it is impossible to make a machine that functions by completely converting heat, drawn from some body or object at a given temperature, into work (in the sense of physics, where a force moves something over a distance). This is one of the most important constraints of physics. A lot of heat is generated by friction, for example; this is wasteful, for more effort is required in the presence of friction than without it. What the second law of thermodynamics says is that some of this loss is not reversible.

Consider pushing a cart across a level street, an example discussed in the earlier sidebar, "The First Law of Thermodynamics." Pushing a cart involves work, but unlike lifting a weight, there is little or no energy "stored" in the position of the cart—it cannot return across the street on its own or do work in the process. Friction and air resistance generates heat, and although the energy of motion that produces this heat is not destroyed, the conversion is not fully reversible. Some of this thermal energy can be used to do work, but not all. No matter how the attempt is made or what machine or technology is employed, it is not possible to recapture all of the thermal energy and do work with it.

Getting around the second law of thermodynamics would be terrific because then it would be possible to do such things as moving heat from a cold body to a hot one without any energy input. Air-conditioning would be free. It is not, however, and can never be, because plenty of careful experiments involving heat and work confirm that the world adheres to the second law of thermodynamics.

There are several formulations of the second law of thermodynamics. Chapter 5 describes one that is different but equivalent to the above.

under low pressure, it evaporates and becomes a gas, which then expands. This cools the fluid in the same way that a breath blown through compressed lips feels cool—although the air comes from the body, which is warm, as the air leaves the compressed lips, it expands. The molecules of the gas lose energy as they expand because they push away the surrounding air molecules, thus doing work on them. According to the first law of thermodynamics, some of their energy is lost. As a result, the temperature falls.

The evaporator is located inside. As the working fluid cools, it absorbs heat from the room. This lowers the temperature of the room. But the fluid must deposit this heat outside or the job is not finished.

The working fluid, which is now a warm, low-pressure gas, circulates through pipes and enters a compressor. The compressor does what its name suggests: it compresses the gas by application of pressure. This requires work (and therefore energy) because it forces the fluid to go into a small space.

The compression rapidly increases the temperature of the working fluid. There is a law, called the ideal gas law, that neatly describes this process with an equation relating volume, pressure, and temperature of a gas. The temperature increase can also be thought of in the following way. During the compression, the walls of the chamber holding the gaseous atoms and molecules move inward (similar to a bad horror movie in which the walls start to

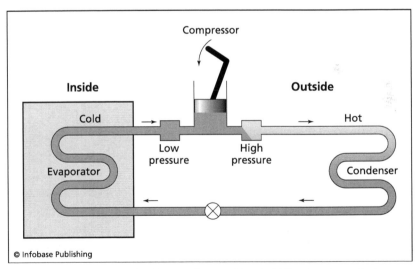

The cooling process transfers heat with a working fluid flowing through the pipe. On the inside, the fluid picks up heat by evaporation (a phase transition from liquid to gas) and expansion. After compression, the fluid loses this heat to the outside by condensing (a phase transition from gas to liquid).

cave in). The atoms and molecules are always in motion, and when they bounce off the inward moving wall, they gain a little more speed from the impact. (If the wall was moving outward, they would lose a little speed.) Temperature depends on atomic and molecular speed, and the fluid gets warmer.

Now the gas is hot, and it circulates to the condenser—a long, thin metal tube, like the evaporator, except the condenser is located outside. If the working fluid is hotter than the outside air, then heat flows out of it though the metal tube (which is an effective heat conductor). Thermal energy escapes, and the working fluid condenses into a liquid. When the fluid emerges from the condenser, it has changed from a hot, high-pressure gas to a warm liquid and has transferred heat from the inside to the outside. From here the liquid returns to evaporator, and the cycle begins again.

Heat flows in its natural direction both inside and outside the room during the operation of the air conditioner. But a little manipulation of the working fluid made it cooler than the room temperature (so heat flows in) and warmer than the outside temperature (so heat flows out). This required compression of the working fluid, which is the part of the process that needs energy, usually in the form of electricity to operate the machine.

The working fluid could be water, but in general it is not. For a long time after people first developed air conditioners, the fluid was a substance called a chlorofluorocarbon (CFC), which contains chlorine atoms. This substance is an excellent choice because it makes phase transitions between gas and liquid over a wide range of temperatures. It is also cheap and does not corrode the air conditioner's pipes and tubes. The problem is that CFCs sometimes release chlorine atoms, which enter the atmosphere and attack the ozone layer. The ozone layer is essential for the protection of life on the planet because it absorbs harmful ultraviolet radiation from the Sun. Recently, CFCs have been replaced by hydrofluorocarbons, which do not contain chlorine. These substances do not work as well as chlorofluorocarbons, but they seem to be safer for the ozone layer. (However, they happen to be greenhouse gases, as mentioned in chapter 1.)

Refrigerators perform the same kind of operation as air conditioners, except they do not cool the room or a house but rather the small area of the refrigerator's interior, where food and other perishables are kept. As in air conditioners, a circulating fluid in the refrigerator extracts heat from the interior and deposits it elsewhere. In the case of refrigerators, "elsewhere" means not outside the room or house but rather outside the refrigerator; generally, this means the heat goes into the room.

A hand placed behind the refrigerator will discover the heat flowing from the working fluid as it circulates in the condenser coils. (The coils are the grill-like objects at the back of the refrigerator.) Because the refrigerator transfers heat into the room, it is not a good idea to try to use it as an air conditioner by leaving the door open. Although the frigid air from the refrigerator's interior will temporarily cool a person standing next to the open door, the room will not get any cooler. When the door is open, the refrigerator will continue to run, taking heat from inside the refrigerator—which, with the door open, is the entire room—and depositing it back into the room. This is no way to run an air conditioner!

Reversible Heat Pumps

Air conditioners are sometimes called heat pumps because they pump heat from the inside of a room or house to the outside. This cools the inside and makes the outside a little bit warmer, though not warm enough to make much of a difference. (But as discussed in the section on the urban heat island effect, a huge number of air conditioners operating at the same time, as in a large city, might have an impact on the city's temperature.)

In the winter, people do not need to cool the house, but rather keep it warm. The traditional manner of doing this is by using a heater. But over the last few decades, engineers and scientists have started looking at another option. What if an air conditioner could be made to work in the reverse direction? Then it would pump heat from the outside to the inside. The result is that the temperature inside would rise.

Similar to air-conditioning, this kind of heat pump would require energy, because during the winter it would be moving heat from the cold exterior to a warmer interior, in opposition to heat's natural flow. But the idea is exactly the same as air-conditioning, and the same procedure would work. All that is needed is to reverse the circulation of the working fluid.

Many homes and businesses are choosing reversible heat pumps to maintain year-round comfortable temperatures. (Some people simply call these devices heat pumps.) They are not the same as air conditioners because they must be reversible. There is not much advantage of a reversible heat pump over a traditional (one-way) air conditioner, because they work the same way; the advantage is that heat pumps prevent the need for installing both an air conditioner and a conventional furnace or heater. Furthermore, heat pumps are usually more efficient heaters. Although extracting heat from the cold air outside and moving it to the inside of the house requires energy, it does not generally require as much as the burning of oil and gas or sending a lot of electrical current through a heating element.

The problem with reversible heat pumps is that in the winter they sometimes need to be run in air-conditioner mode for brief periods of time. This is particularly necessary when the temperature goes below freezing, because ice can form on the coils outside. To keep from blowing cold air into the house, the machine uses heating elements to warm the air during these short periods when it is running in the wrong direction. Although these periods of time do not last very long, they cut down on the overall efficiency of the heat pump.

An excellent way of getting the most out of heat pumps would be to have access to a gigantic object that is at a relatively constant temperature throughout the year, neither very cold in winter nor very warm in summer. A heat pump could efficiently draw heat from the object during winter and deposit heat during the summer. Due to its size, the object would not change temperature much in the process, so it would provide a nearly inexhaustible source of heat in the winter and a heat "sink" or "drain" during the summer. This source surprisingly exists. It is called Earth.

The Earth's interior is hot, as volcano eruptions repeatedly demonstrate. The center of Earth is about 4,000 miles (6,400 km) below the surface, and geologists believe that its temperature is about 7,000°F (3,870°C). (Though no one knows for sure, because no one has been able to measure the temperature at Earth's center directly.) Heat flows upward toward the cooler crust. The soil not far below the surface has a nearly constant temperature—it is in thermal equilibrium, balanced by heat from below and the cold, exposed surface layer of dirt and rocks. The temperature of this subsurface region depends on latitude (north-south location), ranging from 50–70°F (10–21.1°C).

Heat pumps that take advantage of this source are called geothermal heat pumps (*geo* refers to Earth). They should become more common in the future. Thermodynamics places strict limitations on the manner by which people can heat and cool homes, so everyone needs to take advantage of any opportunity to increase efficiency.

Absolute Zero

Heat pumps use energy to take away heat from one object, which gets cooler, and deposit it in another object, which gets warmer. But it is not possible to keep doing this forever, for there is a limit to how much heat can be taken away from an object.

The coldest possible temperature, absolute zero, represents this limit. This temperature, which is designated 0 K in the absolute scale, -459.69°F in the Fahrenheit scale, and −273.15°C in the Celsius scale, is the lowest possible temperature for any object. As mentioned earlier, this is the temperature in which the motion of the atoms and molecules is at a minimum.

Another way of looking at absolute zero is that it is the point at which no further heat energy can be extracted from the body. No matter how hard the pump tries, no more heat will flow.

Absolute zero is the subject of the *third law of thermodynamics*. This law, like the other laws of thermodynamics, is restrictive, because the third law describes something people will never be able to do. The third law of thermodynamics says that not only is

The *Spitzer Space Telescope,* launched on August 25, 2003, is seen here in preparation. The orbiting telescope detects and images infrared radiation, and some of its instruments must be cooled to within a few degrees of absolute zero to avoid interfering signals from their own radiation. Liquid helium is the coolant. *(NASA)*

absolute zero the coldest possible temperature, but no one can ever get an object to even reach this temperature. Nature will simply not allow this to happen. Physicists can cool an object to a temperature that is extremely close to absolute zero, and there is no limit to how close they can come. But absolute zero can never be attained.

Cooling objects to within a few billionths of a degree above absolute zero is possible, but is difficult to do. Heat flows from high to low temperatures, and anything that is close to absolute zero is a lot colder than everything else in the environment. Scientists who study very cold temperatures must do their research in special laboratories. Even with complex equipment, it is hard to stop heat from seeping into a frigid object and raising its temperature. Conduction and convection are heat transfer mechanisms that can be controlled to a great extent, but radiation is not easy to stop. Materials cooled to temperatures close to absolute zero are usually tiny in size and must be placed in special containers.

Despite the problems, there is a lot of incentive for physicists to study objects with temperatures near absolute zero. The properties of matter only a few degrees above absolute zero can be remarkably strange and enormously useful. Dutch physicist Heike Kamerlingh Onnes (1853–1926) discovered superconductivity—the loss of all resistance to the flow of electrical current—in a 1911 experiment in which he cooled mercury to about four degrees above absolute zero. Physicists have since discovered materials that become superconductors at higher temperatures, although still not quite warm enough for these superconductors to be practical for everyday usage.

Another cold and unusual object is space itself. It might be surprising that empty space has a temperature. Space is mostly a vacuum; there are extremely few atoms and molecules, and therefore little atomic and molecular motion. There is, however, a lot of radiation, and space has a well-defined temperature. That temperature is not absolute zero but is close, about –458.8°F (–270.45°C or 2.7 K).

Why does space have this particular temperature? Physicists believe that this energy—the radiation that fills space—is leftover from the cataclysmic "big bang" in which the universe was born, 14 billion years ago. The energy is like the warmth in a chimney after the fire has gone out; this temperature, though only a few degrees above absolute zero, is the remainder of the explosion that created the universe so long ago.

An object placed in space far away from any star or planet would eventually come to a thermal equilibrium with space, attaining a temperature of –458.8°F (–270.45°C or 2.7 K). But cooling an object on Earth to this temperature requires a great deal of effort, moving heat against its natural flow and preventing it from returning. Refrigerators and air conditioners can do the job, but as the temperature of the object drops, the cooling equipment must work against an increasing temperature difference—this means that the "hill" gets steeper. Powerful equipment and special material that can handle such cold temperatures must be used.

Moving heat from cold objects to warm ones takes a great deal of ingenuity. The laws of thermodynamics are not much help, since they enforce strict constraints on what is possible. But knowledge of these laws prevents society from wasting time and money on equipment that has no hope of ever working. People employ technology to maintain a comfortable temperature, even in extreme environments. This technology works well, but the physics of thermodynamics indicates there will always be a cost involved.

4

HEAT ENGINES

A S THEY ROAR around a track at speeds of 200 miles per hour (320 km/hr.), race cars demonstrate the power of heat engines. Jet airplanes soaring in the sky, ships moving through water, and passenger cars traveling down the road are other examples of the utility of heat engines. Heat engines are everywhere, and their usefulness does not come from any complex principle but is instead due to the simple ability of an expanding gas to do work. The basic process is so strongly rooted in thermodynamics that people discovered many of the ideas of thermodynamics by studying and thinking about heat engines.

A heat engine is a machine that converts thermal energy into work, putting vehicles in motion or raising heavy objects. The heat comes from some sort of combustion (burning) process. Not every engine is a heat engine—some engines use electricity—but the basis for the beginning of the Industrial Revolution in the late 18th and early 19th centuries was the heat engine, and it will still be around well into the foreseeable future.

But heat engines have not remained constant—they have evolved over time. The Bell X-1, the plane with which Chuck Yeager broke the sound barrier in 1947, and race driver Jeff Gordon's car were not developed in the earliest years of the Industrial Revolution. Although the fundamental thermodynamics has remained

A powerful engine launches this Titan IV Centaur rocket at Vandenberg Air Force Base, California. *(United States Air Force)*

the same, the specific mechanisms and parts of heat engines have not. *Steam engines* came first.

Steam Power

Miners have always had problems with flooding, and in 1698 British engineer Thomas Savery (1650–1715) constructed what was probably the first steam engine, which was used to pump water.

Another British engineer, Thomas Newcomen (1663–1729), developed a steam engine in the early 1700s that would become the forerunner of most of the later, more efficient machines. Newcomen's engine used a device called a piston.

In an ordinary steam engine, the piston is like a plunger that fits snugly in a cylinder, as shown in the figure on page 74. Steam from a boiler enters the cylinder in one direction and exerts pressure—a force acting over an area—on the piston, moving it forward. The moving piston pushes a jointed rod that has two parts. The part connected to the piston is called the connecting rod, and the other part is called the crankshaft and is attached to a heavy wheel, the flywheel. As the piston moves, the connecting rod and crankshaft transfer this motion into a rotation of the flywheel.

The piston can only move so far in the cylinder and soon reaches the limit—this is one stroke of the piston. If all the engine could accomplish is one little push, it would not be very useful, so when the forward motion is finished, the piston must back up and go through the same process again. But there is a problem: the steam that pushed the piston forward is still around, making it difficult for the piston to back up. Early steam engines cooled the cylinder, and the steam turned back into water, so there was no more pressure against the piston. But this meant the cylinder had to be reheated in order for steam to initiate the next stroke of the piston. James Watt (1736–1819), a Scottish engineer, realized it would be much better if the steam simply escaped. He developed valves to let steam enter the cylinder (through the inlet valve) and to escape (through the exhaust valve) when the piston was ready to come back. Although Watt did not invent the steam engine, his improvements were necessary to make the steam engine efficient enough to power the Industrial Revolution.

The steam comes from the boiler, a sturdy metal container that holds a quantity of water. The burning of some kind of fuel, such as coal or wood, raises the temperature of the water past the boiling point, producing steam—hot water vapor.

Why steam and not something else? Steam is effective because of its high energy; it contains the energy that was put into the sys-

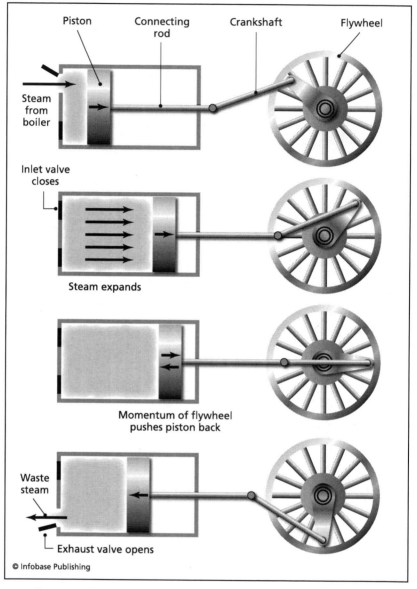

Piston | Connecting rod | Crankshaft | Flywheel

Steam from boiler

Inlet valve closes

Steam expands

Momentum of flywheel pushes piston back

Waste steam

Exhaust valve opens

© Infobase Publishing

Expanding steam enters a steam engine's cylinder and pushes the piston forward. A connecting rod and crankshaft link the piston to a wheel, the flywheel, whose rotation does work such as operate a pump or spin an axle.

tem to raise the temperature of the water, as well as the energy to raise the temperature of the steam. Water boils at 212°F (100°C) and so steam is initially at this temperature, but with additional heat the temperature of steam can be raised, in which case it is sometimes referred to as superheated steam.

Chapter 1 described heat as a flow of energy related to the motion of atoms and molecules. Higher temperatures mean that the atomic and molecular components of a substance are flying around or vibrating faster and with more energy. Some of this energy can be converted into work, which is what a heat engine does. But steam also has another source of energy—the latent heat of vaporization. As discussed in chapter 3, energy is required to break bonds holding atoms or molecules together. This is what happens when water is turned into steam, because the bonds holding water molecules together get broken and the molecules go flying off as a gas. The process does not destroy this energy (which is forbidden by the first law of thermodynamics), the energy simply exists as a different form, called the latent heat of vaporization. This is the energy contained by the state or phase of a substance. Water absorbs heat to turn it into steam, but the reverse process—when steam condenses back into water—returns this energy.

Steam can exert an enormous pressure. Water vapor fills a volume of about 1,500 times greater than the same amount of liquid at normal pressure (the pressure of Earth's atmosphere). This pressure can do work, which is defined in physics as exerting a force over a distance. In steam engines, the steam does work on the piston. But this work does not come free, because the first law of thermodynamics says that a system loses energy when heat flows out of it or when it does work. When steam pushes against the piston, it does work, so it loses energy. As a consequence, its temperature falls—the motion of its water molecules is "spent" doing this work. The boiler must replace this energy, which means the boiler must be kept going. Fuel is needed to keep the boiler hot. Without fuel the steam engine, or any heat engine, stops working.

Heat engines such as steam engines are similar to the heat pumps discussed earlier, except they run in opposite directions. Air conditioners and refrigerators are heat engines run backwards, as illustrated in the diagram on page 76. (A similar situation exists in electricity: an electric motor is an electric generator running in reverse.)

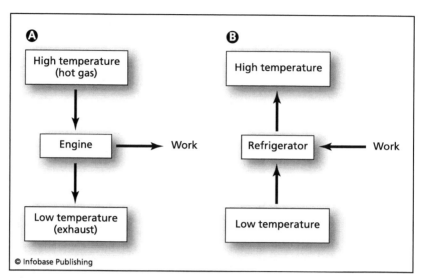

A heat engine and a refrigerator are two different machines. But box diagrams for both of these machines show their relationship—the engine does work from the "downhill" movement of heat from hot temperatures to cold (A), and refrigerators and air conditioners move heat "uphill" with the help of work done by electricity (B).

How much work a steam engine can do depends on several factors. Important factors include the average pressure, the area of the piston and the distance it moves, and how many strokes occur per minute. Further development of steam engines occurred as engineers squeezed all the power they could get out of these machines. Watt took the big step, but steam engines continued to be refined. Better efficiency meant less fuel to do a given amount of work, saving the operator money.

But the subject of thermodynamics seems full of limits—the first, second, and third laws of thermodynamics are often phrased in terms of something that cannot be accomplished—so there is reason to suspect the existence of a limit to the efficiency of a steam engine (or any heat engine). Much to the chagrin of engineers all over the world, such a limit exists.

But an understanding of the efficiency limit of heat engines produced a great deal of insight. (Some people say that it even gave rise to the science of thermodynamics.) British scientist James Joule

(1818–89) showed that a given amount of work always produces a certain amount of heat, and his experiments were important in formulating the first law of thermodynamics. But when people wondered if the opposite was true—whether a given amount of heat always produces a certain amount of work—the answer, to the dismay of efficiency-seeking engineers, was no.

Heat cannot be completely converted into work. This is the idea behind the second law of thermodynamics, as described earlier. This means that some heat—some energy, in other words—must be wasted in a heat engine. But how much energy must be wasted? Efficiency requires as little waste as possible, so the question becomes one of finding the maximum efficiency of a heat engine. As described in the following sidebar, French engineer and scientist Sadi Carnot (1796–1832) found the answer, not by tinkering with steam engines, but rather by sitting down and thinking about the underlying physics. His ideas apply not just to steam engines but to all heat engines.

According to Carnot, given the temperature, T_h, of the heat source and the temperature, T_l, of the exhaust environment, the best efficiency, E, that any kind of heat engine can achieve is $E = 1 - T_l / T_h$ (the temperatures must be in the absolute scale). An efficiency of 1 means that all heat is converted into work, but Carnot's equation means that no heat engine can possibly ever reach this mark. In the process of converting heat into work, some of the heat must be exhausted into the environment. All heat engines waste some of their fuel by uselessly exhausting some of the energy into the environment. This cannot be avoided.

Carnot's theory is true, but it puzzled scientists for many years. No one could figure out why physics requires some heat to be wasted in the exhaust of a heat engine. It seems almost mean-spirited, as if nature was thumbing its nose at engineers who are always striving to improve their machines. The reasons for Carnot's theory involve a strange and interesting concept called *entropy*, to be discussed in the next chapter of this volume.

Although Carnot's theory was not what engineers wanted to hear, it was an advance in physics and important to know for anyone designing a heat engine. The best that an engineer can do is make

The Carnot Engine

Sadi Carnot had a major impact on the development of thermodynamics as a branch of physics. Trained as a military engineer, Carnot later turned his attention to the analysis of heat engines. Carnot was a theorist—he was not interested in building engines but in understanding how they function. Although Carnot did not understand heat very well, he had an excellent grasp of engineering principles, and he started his analysis with a correct assumption, probably based on hard experience. Carnot assumed there was no such thing as a free lunch—he assumed that an engine could not create energy out of nothing. He also observed that heat always flows "downhill"—from hot to cold objects—and he reasoned that heat engines operate somewhat like waterwheels. In a waterwheel, the water does work by falling from a high place to a lower one, turning the wheel in the process. In Carnot's analysis, heat flowed from a higher temperature to a lower temperature and did work in the process.

Carnot simplified his analysis by excluding energy losses from friction or from heat escaping from the cylinder as the hot gas expanded. In other words, the engine behaved perfectly. The heat engine that he considered—today called a *Carnot engine* in his honor—is an ideal engine, as good as it can possibly be. Carnot analyzed the piston stroke as a cycle, with the heat input

the temperature, T_h, of the heat source to be much higher than the temperature, T_l, of the exhaust environment. In this case the ratio T_l/T_h is a small quantity—T_l is low, and T_h is high. But an engineer must remember that Carnot's engine is ideal—a real heat engine will also suffer from losses due to friction and heat escaping from the cylinder, so the theoretical efficiency is a ceiling that can never actually be reached. Another problem is that the nature of the fuel and exhaust environment—commonly beyond the control of engineers—often dictate the operating temperatures of a heat engine.

Despite these problems, heat engines became popular. In the early years, steam engines performed many jobs, such as pumping water out of mines or powering ships or trains. Steam engines were easy to build and they worked well at low speeds, so they were perfect for massive locomotives. Wood or coal provided the fuel.

coming from a large heat source at temperature, T_h, and the exhaust going into a "sink" that has a temperature, T_l. He calculated the efficiency of this ideal engine.

Efficiency is important because it represents how much work one can get out of an input of energy. Poor efficiency costs an enormous amount of money. The efficiency of a heat engine is the work done divided by the heat that it "absorbed" (in other words, the heat that was converted into work). The first law of thermodynamics limits the efficiency to be no greater than 1—in this case all of the heat energy does work. But Carnot found that the best possible efficiency, E, is less than 1 and is given by the equation

$$E = 1 - T_l / T_h,$$

where the units of both temperatures T_l and T_h are the Kelvin (absolute) scale. The temperature, T_h, of the heat source must be greater than the temperature, T_l, of the environment into which the waste is exhausted, otherwise the heat engine will not operate, since heat only flows naturally from high to low temperatures. Therefore the ratio T_l / T_h must be less than 1. But this ratio cannot be zero because T_l cannot be zero: in the Kelvin scale, zero is absolute zero, a temperature that can be approached but never reached (see the earlier section "Absolute Zero" in chapter 3).

Steam power transformed the world and was largely responsible for the Industrial Revolution. The first steam locomotives appeared in the early 19th century and vastly improved trade and transportation. The first transcontinental railroad linking the east and west of the United States was finished in 1869, and soon railroads became the backbone of American business. Steamships regularly plied the waters, such as the SS *California* in the 1840s. (The SS means that the ship was a steamship.)

Steam engines were not limited to big ships or locomotives. In the late 19th century, steam "horseless carriages" built by engineers such as the Stanley brothers appeared. Although some of these Stanley Steamers could go quite fast, most of the models were not so nimble. One steam carriage demonstrated in 1898 could carry two passengers at a maximum speed of about 20 miles per hour (32 km/hr.). Steam carriages were not only slow, they were also loud and required a long time to warm up before they would start going (it took time to heat the boiler, especially on a cold morning). But even though they were not quite as useful as horses, steam carriages were still welcome, especially in large, populous cities. Horses are a wonderful means of transportation but their exhaust is much worse than that of a steam engine, forcing New York City of the 19th century to deal with 2 million pounds of horse manure and thousands of gallons of urine that littered the streets every day. In that era, the city must have been, to put it mildly, an aromatic place.

Most of the piston-driven steam engines were gradually replaced by another engine, the steam *turbine*. A turbine is a rotating, bladed shaft, similar to a propeller. In a steam turbine, high-pressure steam pushes against the blades, turning the turbine, as shown in the figure below. The motion is rotary, unlike piston-driven steam engines that usually must convert the

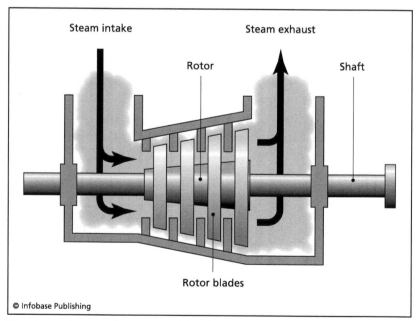

This simple diagram of a steam turbine shows steam entering the engine through the intake and pushing against the blades of a rotor, causing it to turn. The rotor connects with a ship's propeller shaft or some other device.

back-and-forth piston movement into a force that rotates a wheel or shaft.

Steam turbines are excellent engines for ships, providing power for such early 20th-century vessels as the RMS *Mauretania* and RMS *Titanic*. Steam turbines work so well that they are still widely used today (unlike piston steam engines, which are now mostly found in museums and antique collections), powering many of today's ships. Electric utility companies also use steam turbines to generate electricity. This includes power plants employing nuclear energy, since these utilities do not convert nuclear energy directly into electricity but instead use the nuclear energy to produce steam, which drives a turbine. The motion of the turbine, along with some electrical apparatus, generates the electricity.

Another kind of heat engine became prominent in the early 20th century, and it also helped send the piston steam engine into retirement. A steam engine is an external combustion engine—the combustion that produces the steam occurs in or around the boiler, not in the piston cylinder, so it is external to the cylinder. Engineers began building a piston-driven *internal combustion engine,* in which the combustion to produce the hot, expanding gas occurred not in a boiler but in the cylinder itself. The fuel was a petroleum product,

One of the fastest and largest cruise ships of the 20th century, the SS *United States* ("Big U"), launched in 1952, now lies unused at a dock in Philadelphia, Pennsylvania. *(Kyle Kirkland)*

which when burned produced a hot gas that was not steam but nevertheless did the job of pushing the piston well enough. The internal combustion engine proved so useful for small vehicles that it became by far the most popular engine for cars.

Car Engines

The early internal combustion engines were not perfect, but they had an overwhelming advantage over steam engines that was irresistible to motorists—internal combustion engines were more powerful. Cars with internal combustion engines did not have a heavy boiler, did not require a lot of water, did not need any coal, and, with their powerful engines, they could go fast. When Henry Ford decided to use internal combustion engines in his popular Model T cars in the early 20th century, the other types of engine gradually disappeared.

Passenger cars of today usually have either four, six, or eight cylinders and run on gasoline. The basic process of moving each piston in the cylinder is the same as a steam engine, but of course steam is not used. As shown in the figure on page 83, gasoline and air enter the cylinder through the inlet valve. Air is essential because oxygen must be present for the gasoline to burn. The motion of the piston compresses this air-fuel mixture into the small space between the top of the piston and the edge of the cylinder. The job of igniting the mixture goes to the spark plug, as thousands of volts of electricity arc across a small gap, and the spark ignites the gasoline and oxygen mixture. A small explosion results, creating hot, expanding gas that pushes the cylinder. This is the power stroke: during this movement, the piston delivers a force to the crankshaft, which rotates and produces the power to turn the wheels. (The crankshaft is linked to the wheels by the transmission system.) After the power stroke occurs, another valve—the exhaust valve—opens, and the warm gas goes out of the cylinder, eventually finding its way into the environment through the muffler (which reduces the noise of the explosions) and the tailpipe.

The cylinders of the engine do not all deliver their power stroke at the same time. The pistons work together, and at any given time, some are delivering the power that rotates the crankshaft, and others are getting pushed back into position by the crankshaft's momentum. The timing of the piston movement is important, and

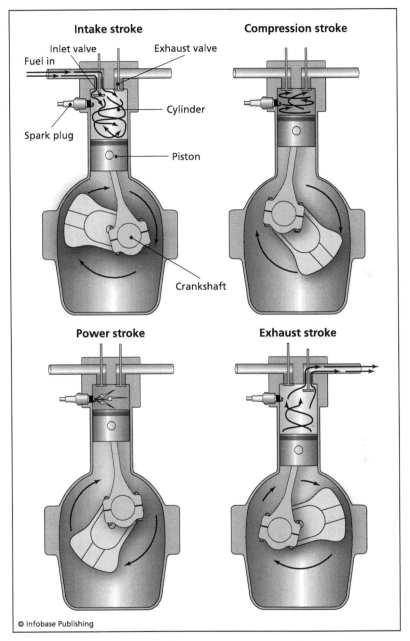

Intake stroke

Fuel in
Inlet valve
Exhaust valve
Spark plug
Cylinder
Piston
Crankshaft

Compression stroke

Power stroke

Exhaust stroke

© Infobase Publishing

Gasoline-powered internal combustion engines are often based on four strokes. The piston descends in the intake stroke as fuel and air enter the cylinder. The compression stroke compresses the air and fuel, and after ignition, the explosion drives the piston down with a great deal of force (power stroke). During the exhaust stroke, the piston ascends and clears the cylinder. The crankshaft's momentum or the work of other cylinders in the engine drives the piston's movement on all strokes except the power stroke.

if it is not right, then the engine will operate inefficiently. In four-cylinder engines, the pistons are usually placed in a row, but such an "in-line" configuration is sometimes too long in engines with more than four cylinders. Six- and eight-cylinder engines often have the piston cylinders arranged in a V-configuration, half on one side of the engine and half on the other, as shown in the figure below. A six-cylinder engine in this arrangement is called a V6 and an eight-cylinder engine a V8.

Most internal combustion engines today are called four-stroke engines because they have four strokes, or parts, to a cycle: (1) intake of the air-fuel mixture, (2) compression of the mixture, (3) explosion and power stroke, and (4) exhaust of the waste gases. The four-stroke cycle uses the ideas of German engineer Nikolaus Otto (1832–91). The earliest internal combustion engines had a cycle of two strokes, but this was not efficient and the exhaust was dirty, often containing unburned fuel. Even so, a lot of small machines today use two-stroke internal combustion engines because they

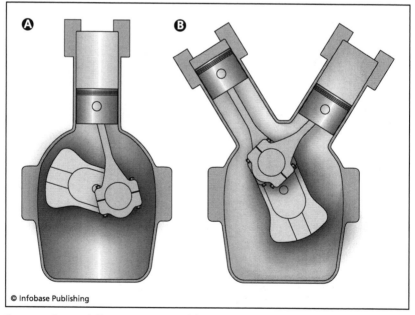

© Infobase Publishing

Compared to an inline arrangement (A), V engines (B) configure the pistons in two rows at an angle, forming the letter V.

can fit into a small space and deliver plenty of power—one of the two strokes is a power stroke, instead of only one of four in the four-stroke cycle. Many scooters and outboard motor boats have two-stroke engines.

The energy to push the pistons comes from the expanding gas of the explosion. In principle, any fuel is acceptable as long as it produces a high-pressure gas that can do work on the piston. As mentioned earlier, steam has a lot of energy and so it can do a lot of work. Gasoline and other, similar fuels, such as diesel, have plenty of energy also, though their energy is not in the same form as steam and comes from their chemistry. The combustion process is a chemical reaction in which the fuel reacts with oxygen to produce other compounds and also releases energy. Chemists call this kind of reaction an exothermic reaction. Steam engines also involve this type of reaction since the energy given off by combustion of wood or coal produced the heat to generate the steam.

Gasoline had been discovered well before the development of internal combustion engines. Crude oil contains many different compounds, and when it is refined—separated into its components—gasoline is one of the products. But before the days of internal combustion engines, crude oil refiners were primarily after kerosene (commonly used in lamps) and other products for lubrication. Refiners considered gasoline worthless and often simply let it burn in air. The appearance of internal combustion engines changed all that, of course.

Internal combustion engines are heat engines and are subject to the laws and limitations of thermodynamics, including Carnot's theory. For example, a car engine might operate at about 5,500°F (3,038°C or 3,311 K) and exhaust the waste gases at a temperature of 2,000°F (1,093°C or 1,366 K). The theoretical limit for this car's efficiency is (using Carnot's equation and Kelvin temperatures) $1 - 1,366/3,311 = 0.587$, or 58.7 percent. This means that at most 58.7 percent of the heat supplied to the engine can be converted into work.

But even modern and relatively efficient car engines do not get very close to the limit. Internal combustion engines of today convert about a third of the heat energy into work. Of the rest of the heat energy, about a third escapes in the exhaust, and the remaining third is wasted in heat losses through the walls of the cylinder. The heat losses are especially vexing. Instead of being converted into the work of driving the pistons, this heat simply makes the engine hotter, which requires circulating coolant and a radiator to carry this heat away and keep the engine's temperature at a reasonable level.

But there are even more conditions that rob the engine of its efficiency. If all of the gasoline does not burn completely, some of its energy is not released. (Another problem with incomplete combustion is that it produces a lot of pollution, because some of the reaction products are hazardous to humans and attack the environment.) With the speed and power needs of most automobiles, there is not sufficient time to let the fuel mixture burn to completion. An explosion and power stroke occurs, then the engine expels the gas in a hurry to get set up for the next power stroke. Sometimes a lack of oxygen also presents difficulties. Near sea level, such as in most of Florida, plenty of oxygen exists, but those who drive high in the mountains may find that their car engine is not so powerful, since atmospheric pressure decreases with height, and on a mountain, there is less air and therefore less oxygen.

Under normal circumstances, the maximum *power* a car engine can produce is often given in *horsepower*. In the language of physics, power is the rate that a machine uses or produces energy. The greater the horsepower, the greater the energy per unit time and thus the greater the work per unit time—more horsepower means more work done in a given period. (The term *horsepower* comes from the days before car engines, when the standard for measuring the rate of energy and work was the horse.) The average passenger car engine can produce about 180 horsepower. This is not to say that it always produces this amount—just that it can, if the driver were to "floor" the gas pedal, which in most situations is not a good idea.

To produce this horsepower, the pistons turn the crankshaft, which rotates at a certain number of revolutions per minute (*rpm*).

The crankshaft of most passenger cars spins at a few thousand rpm during normal operation, as indicated in some cars by a gauge on the dashboard called a tachometer. How fast the crankshaft turns determines the amount of force that can be applied to the drive-shaft and the wheels. In general, the more pistons an engine has, the more power it has.

The amount of movement that the piston makes is also an important factor in the power of an engine, so engines are often described in terms of *displacement*. As a piston moves, it displaces a certain volume, equal to the product of the cross-sectional area of the piston and the distance it moves during the engine's operation. This is important because volume is related to the amount of work done by the piston. The work, W, equals the product of the force, F, of the piston and the distance, d, it moves, and the equation can be written as

$$W = Fd = Fd \frac{A}{A},$$

where A is the cross-sectional area of the piston. The factor A/A does not change the equation because it is unity (the number 1), and multiplying any number by 1 equals that number. Rearranging this equation:

$$W = Fd \frac{A}{A} = \frac{F}{A} \, dA.$$

Since pressure, P, is force, F, over area, A, and volume, V, is the product of distance, d, and area, A,

$$W = \frac{F}{A} \, dA = PV.$$

The pressure of the hot, expanding gas acting on the piston causes it to move through a certain volume—this is the work. (The equation can also be considered as describing the expansion of gas into a certain volume—the formula would be the same.)

The sum of these volumes for all the pistons is the engine's displacement. Engine specifications give the units of displacement in liters, cubic inches, or cubic centimeters (1 liter = 1,000 cubic centimeters = 61 cubic inches). Chevrolet's famous 1967 Camaro SS-350 had an engine with a displacement of 350 cubic inches

(5.74 L). For many years in the 1980s and early 1990s, the top-of-the-line Ford Mustang ran on a 5.0-liter engine—306 cubic inches. These are fairly large displacements compared to most passenger cars.

Cars with powerful engines are sometimes referred to as muscle cars. These engines are built for speed and power, not for efficiency, and there are several ways to make a racing engine out of a heat engine.

Racing Engines

The simplest way to get a powerful heat engine is just to make it bigger. Some of the race cars in the early 20th century had huge displacements compared to modern engines—some were 1,220 cubic inches (20 L) or more, four times the size of a modern muscle car engine! But this size was not necessarily a big advantage. Although the engine is more powerful, it is also much heavier, and a more massive object requires more force to accelerate it. This is because of Newton's second law of motion: the acceleration of an object equals the applied force divided by the mass. For any given force, an object with a lot of mass accelerates much less than an object with little mass. Because of the limits of thermodynamics, only a portion of the heat supplied to the engine can be turned into work, so heat engines are already operating at a disadvantage. Adding to their mass increases the work they have to do, and engine-designers quickly reach a point where making engines bigger does little good.

A similar situation occurs when more pistons are added. Increasing the number of pistons increases the force that can be applied to the crankshaft, which makes the engine more powerful. But the larger number of pistons also increases the engine's mass. Another disadvantage is that adding pistons results in an increase in friction losses, since a greater number of pistons moving and rubbing against the cylinder walls means a greater energy loss due to friction.

An important consideration of pistons is not only their number but also the compression ratio—this measures the extent to which the fuel-air mixture is compressed in the piston cylinder. The compression ratio is the ratio of two volumes—the volume of the cylinder when the piston is at its low point and the volume of the cylinder when the piston is at its high point, as shown in the figure below. If the compression ratio is large, then the fuel-air mixture occupies a small space immediately before the fuel is ignited. Under this kind of high pressure, the hot gas can expand and do more work, so an engine with a higher compression ratio is in principle capable of more power. In practice, though, the compression ratio cannot be made too large without disrupting the fuel ignition and piston timing.

Other options for getting more power out of an internal combustion engine include burning a richer mixture of fuel and air, which increases the amount of hot gases that expand against the piston. More fuel requires more air because the additional fuel requires additional oxygen to support combustion (one of the primary methods of extinguishing a fire is to deprive it of oxygen). The extra air and fuel requires more volume—especially the air,

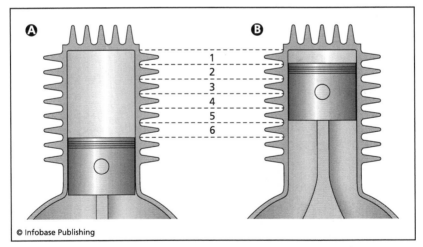

© Infobase Publishing

The compression ratio refers to the amount of volume the piston compresses and is found by comparing the volume of the cylinder when the piston is at the bottom of its motion (A) with the volume when the piston is at the top (B). The volume in (A) is six times the volume in (B), so the compression ratio of this cylinder is 6 to 1.

which is not dense. But the high compression ratio of powerful engines means that the fuel-air mixture does not have a lot of room. The solution to this problem is to make the air dense at the beginning, and this is the job of an engine device called a *supercharger*.

Superchargers are compressors. Their job is to get more oxygen into the piston cylinder by squeezing the air into a small space. Superchargers are also called blowers, because they blow high-pressure air into the engine. The higher amount of oxygen supports a higher level of combustion, increasing the available power. The price to pay for this increased power is the energy needed to run the compressor—nothing comes free in physics, particularly when thermodynamics is involved. The supercharger's compressor usually gets its energy from the rotation of the crankshaft, and this slows down the crankshaft by a small amount. But the increased oxygen in the cylinder more than makes up for the loss.

Another way to increase the amount of air entering the cylinder is to use a *turbocharger*. The job of a turbocharger is similar to a supercharger, compressing the air before it gets into the cylinder. But turbochargers do not rob the crankshaft of any of its power since they get their energy from the engine's exhaust gases. When exiting the engine, the exhaust gases turn a fan or a turbine that runs the compressor.

Turbochargers are common in cars and trucks today, for both diesel engines and gasoline-powered cars. German car manufacturer Porsche is well known for its turbocharged vehicles. But although turbochargers do not rob the crankshaft of power, they do have a disadvantage over superchargers in that they operate with a time lag. When the driver presses the car's accelerator quickly, the turbocharger responds with a delay—because exhaust is involved, a turbocharger cannot act immediately.

People have used all of these methods—bigger engines, more pistons, turbocharging, and supercharging—to make race-car engines. But today many race cars do not use any of these methods, and professional racing organizations specify the size and properties of the engines that are permitted to compete in the races, making for a fair contest. Race cars known as Formula One

A NASCAR race car zooms along the track at the Las Vegas Motor Speedway. *(U.S. Air Force/Master Sgt. Robert W. Valenca)*

cars must have a V10 engine with a displacement of 3,000 cubic centimeters—183 cubic inches. This is not a big engine, yet the top Formula One race cars can reach speeds of 220 miles per hour (350 km/hr.)! The popular racing organization NASCAR uses eight-cylinder engines with a specified displacement of about 350 cubic inches (5.74 liters or 5,740 cubic centimeters).

The enormous power of today's race cars come from high compression ratios, rich fuels, and an ability to run at an amazing rpm—the crankshaft of some of the best Formula One racers approach a spin rate of 20,000 rpm (333 revolutions each second!). These race cars are fast because the engines take in air and burn fuel at an exceptionally high rate. This means that the pistons must be moving remarkably fast, and in some race cars, the pistons experience acceleration forces as great as 9,000 times gravity. This is why the crankshaft turns at such a high rpm, which delivers a huge amount of energy to the wheels.

As mentioned earlier, most ordinary cars operate at a few thousand rpm. Twenty thousand rpm generates so much rotational force and so much heat from friction that ordinary passenger cars would melt or fall apart. Race cars such as Formula One cars have to be made from special metal alloys and other materials that can withstand the friction and other forces involved with engine speeds of 333 revolutions every second. Even so, most race-car engines must be rebuilt after every race, because many of the parts cannot last long under these extreme conditions. (Some engines do not even manage to last a whole race—engine failure is a common reason that drivers drop out of a race.) Rebuilding an engine is expensive, since they cost about $100,000. These engines are expensive to operate for another reason—a poor fuel mileage of about four miles (6.44 km) per gallon.

Manufacturers of powerful engines also place an emphasis on several other design features, such as the valves for inlets and outlets in the cylinders, the camshaft placement (the camshaft opens the valves), and the mechanism that pumps fuel into the cylinders.

But the fastest land cars in existence today are not piston engines. As of early 2006, the speed record for a car traveling on the ground is 763 miles per hour (1,221 km/hr.), set by Thrust-SSC in October 1997 at the Black Rock Desert in Nevada. (SSC is an abbreviation for Supersonic Car, and the car did manage to achieve supersonic speed—it broke the sound barrier, the first and so far only car to do so.) Speeds of this magnitude require a long, flat surface for a track, such as a salt flat, or a dry lake bed like the Black Rock Desert, one of the flattest surfaces on the Earth. Attaining these speeds also requires much engineering skill, a brave driver, and a lot of physics. The engines are similar to those used to travel in air or space rather than the piston engines that power modern automobiles.

Jet Engines and Gas Turbines

People associate jets with high speed and for good reason—jets power ThrustSSC as well as the fastest airplanes. Like the engines that propel rockets through space, *jet engines* use Newton's third law, which says that for every action there is a reaction. In the case of jets (and rockets), the action is a spewing of gaseous

This 1953 photo shows some of the fast jet airplanes tested by the National Advisory Committee for Aeronautics (NACA, the predecessor of NASA). The airplane in the center is the X-3, and the others are, starting from left and going clockwise, X-1A, D-558-1, XF-92A, X-5, D-558-2, and X-4. *(NASA)*

molecules out the back of the engine. The backward momentum of the gas imparts a forward momentum on the craft—this is the reaction.

The two engines that propelled ThrustSSC to the land speed record were jet engines of the same type that propel military fighter planes. The heart of a jet engine is a heat engine called a gas turbine, and it works on the same thermodynamics principles as the old steam engines and the piston engines that run in most of today's automobiles. The gas turbine is an internal combustion engine that burns a fuel—propane or jet fuel—and uses the hot expanding gas to rotate a turbine. The process is similar to the steam turbine described above.

A basic gas turbine has three parts: a compressor, a combustion chamber, and the turbine, as shown in the figure on page 94. In the combustion chamber, the fuel burns and produces the hot, energetic gas that rotates the turbine. The rotation of the turbine can do work, just like the rotation of a steam turbine or the rotation of a crankshaft in a piston engine, and the work of the turbine is to drive the compressor. Gas turbines use a compressor in a way similar to the piston engines that use high compression ratios and, occasionally, turbochargers or superchargers to increase power. Fuel combustion at normal (atmospheric) pressure produces weak gases that do not expand much, and therefore cannot do much work. Compressing the fuel and air mixture into a small space and then burning it produces a hot, expanding gas at high pressure that can do a lot of work.

In a jet engine, the high-pressure gas not only turns the turbine but also provides thrust. The gas passes through a nozzle and out the back of the engine at high speed. But gas turbines are not just limited to jet airplanes. Gas turbines also power fast ships and drive the motion needed to produce electricity in electric power plants. For these applications, the turbine's rotation drives the main shaft directly, as in a steam turbine. Instead of being channeled through a nozzle, the exhaust gases are simply vented outside, like a muffler and pipe system of a car.

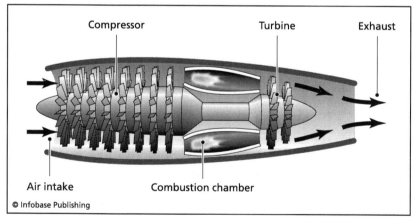

Compressor   Turbine   Exhaust

Air intake   Combustion chamber

© Infobase Publishing

A gasoline turbine is similar to a steam turbine (compare to the figure on page 80), but the energy comes from the burning of gasoline in the combustion chamber. The oxygen to support combustion comes from the intake, and a compressor squeezes the volume of air so that more will fit into the chamber. The hot, expanding gases from the combustion turn the turbine.

Gas turbines are lighter and typically more powerful than piston engines. Large commercial airplanes are powered by jet engines, often seen hanging down from the wings. Many of these gas turbines have an additional component to the three parts already discussed: there is a fan mounted at the initial stage of the engine, which an observer can easily see when viewing the engine from the front. Powered by the turbine's rotation, the fan increases the amount of air taken into the engine and provides more air for thrust.

Although gas turbines are generally more powerful than piston engines, piston engines are still common. The reason for this is the same as why piston engines appeared long before gas turbines. The turbine is not a recent idea—although people developed the jet engine in the 1930s and 1940s, the concept of a turbine goes back to the 18th century. One of the problems with making a high-speed gas turbine involves the design of a compressor strong enough to handle the job. Another big problem was that unlike a piston engine, in which periodic combustions provide a power stroke, a gas turbine continuously burns fuel to rotate the turbine, and it operates under high pressures and temperatures, which puts a lot of stress on its components. Like a race car engine operating at high rpm, jet engines must be made from special materials to withstand the constant heat and pressure. Before jet engines could become a reality, these materials had to be discovered or designed. They are not cheap, so gas turbines are generally too expensive to put into ordinary automobiles.

Carnot's equation says that an increase in operating temperature results in an increase in efficiency for any heat engine. The materials in jet engines can withstand high temperatures, so this is an advantage in terms of thermodynamics. But the efficiency of a gas turbine decreases if it has to stop and start—gas turbines are meant to provide continuous thrust, as they do in jet engines, or continuously turn a heavy object, as they do in electric power plants. This is yet another reason why cars do not use gas turbines, because while highway driving would be fine, the stop-and-go of city traffic would eliminate the gas turbine's advantage.

Although efficiency is important, power and speed are often a jet engine's main concerns. The power can be increased even

Air force maintenance personnel test a jet engine and its afterburner. *(United States Air Force/2nd Lt. Albert Bosco)*

further by adding an afterburner, at the expense of decreased efficiency. An afterburner adds extra fuel to the exhaust and then ignites it, increasing the temperature and velocity of the exhaust, which increases the thrust. This process burns a lot more fuel and reduces the engine's efficiency, but for a fighter pilot trying to out-maneuver an enemy, the extra power is worth the expense.

Heat Engines of the Future

Heat engines have come a long way from the slow, awkward steam engines of the 18th and 19th centuries. Smaller parts, better fuel, and superior materials have produced engines powerful enough to propel cars and airplanes to breathtaking speeds. Although engines of the future will continue to be restricted by the laws of thermodynamics—no engine will ever be able to convert 100 percent of its heat input into work—there is still room for improvement.

Fighter pilots and other people who need to get from one place to another in a hurry never seem to be satisfied—they always want engines with more power and speed. The problem, though, is temperature.

The F-15, a fighter jet of the United States Air Force, can reach a speed of 1,660 miles per hour (2,656 km/hr.), and the SR-71 can fly at close to 2,000 miles per hour (3,200 km/hr.). Flying at even greater speeds than this presents several difficulties. One difficulty is that friction with the air causes the exposed surfaces of the plane to overheat. Another difficulty is the jet engine's compressor; at

The SR-71, an air force plane used in the 1970s and 1980s for reconnaissance missions, was the world's fastest and highest-flying airplane during its years of service. (United States Air Force/Tech. Sgt. Michael Haggerty)

high speed, the temperature of the compressor becomes so hot that it begins to melt.

Afterburners add extra power but also create a disadvantage in terms of military combat. The addition of burning fuel in the exhaust of an airplane with an afterburner will increase the temperature, which is undesirable because it creates a "heat signature" that can be easily detected by a heat-seeking missile (a missile designed to locate its target by sensing the high temperatures of the enemy's airplanes). The afterburner is an excellent target for a heat-seeking missile, and the result could be disastrous for a pilot. For this reason, the United States Air Force wants its future jets to be able to produce a lot of power without having to turn on an afterburner. The F/A-22 Raptor, the newest air force fighter, has this ability, and its two Pratt & Whitney engines produce more thrust than any previous fighter engine. The F/A-22 can cruise at a speed of one-and-a-half times the speed of sound, without engaging the afterburner.

Problems associated with the compressor's high temperature can be partially solved by keeping it cool with a circulating fluid, creating convection currents. Another way is to find new metal alloys to withstand even higher temperatures without melting. Yet

The F/A-22 Raptor (also known as the F-22) is the newest jet fighter in the air force. *(United States Air Force/Tech. Sgt. Ben Bloker)*

another way is to get rid of the compressor entirely. But high pressures are mandatory in order for the engine to do a lot of work, as mentioned earlier, and if the compressor is gone, what will compress the air? The answer is simple—the air itself.

When a jet airplane is traveling at an exceptionally high speed, the compressor gets so hot that it cannot function, but at these high speeds, the air rushes into the engine with a great deal of force anyway. A careful arrangement of the engine inlet can funnel the incoming air and use the air's own momentum to compress it. In this way, a high-enough pressure occurs without a machine compressor. An engine that uses this idea is called a ramjet—the air rams itself into the engine, achieving high pressure.

Ramjets obviously must be going at high speeds before they become usable. The minimum required speed is about 300 miles per hour (484 km/hr.), and most ramjets only become efficient at about twice that speed. The ramjet engine is an extremely simple heat engine, consisting of a long tube in which fuel is burned in the compressed air. Ramjets work quite well at supersonic speeds, although the air is slowed down as it goes through the engine. An even more powerful engine at supersonic speeds is the scramjet (supersonic combustion ramjet), which is a ramjet engine that allows air to travel through the engine at supersonic speed—a lot of compression is available with this kind of speed!

Ramjets and scramjets have been built, but they are still being developed and are not quite ready for everyday use. The National Aeronautics and Space Administration (NASA) tested a scramjet in an unmanned experimental aircraft called X-43A in November 2004. A larger plane carried the attached X-43A aloft; when the operator remotely launched the X-43A, it used a rocket to gain enough speed for the scramjet to function. The scramjet's fuel was hydrogen. Eventually, the aircraft reached a record speed (for this type of engine) of 7,000 miles per hour (11,200 km/hr.). Although the X-43A flew at high altitudes where the air is thin, the speed was so fast that the plane experienced a great deal of friction as it moved through the air. This friction generated so much heat that the craft required circulating water as a coolant to keep from melting.

This drawing shows the X-43A Hypersonic Experimental Vehicle in flight. *(NASA)*

Heat engine development will not stop with scramjets. Speed is not the only important aspect of engines—efficiency is also important. The laws of thermodynamics place strict limits on the ability of heat engines to convert heat into work, and all heat engines must obey these laws no matter what fuel they burn or how they burn it. But even modern heat engines such as the internal combustion engines in automobiles fall well short of Carnot's ideal engine because of heat losses from conduction, convection, and radiation. If heat engines of the future are to wring out all possible work for a given input of energy, they must be made from strong insulators and heat-resistant materials, designed with thermodynamic principles in mind.

5

TIME

THE STUDY OF thermodynamics is critical for understanding heat and temperature, and thermodynamic principles are important in the operation, and limitations, of the many heat engines existing today. But thermodynamics is also critical for another topic—time—which at first seems unrelated.

Everyone is aware of time. People associate time with clocks and with the passing of day into night and night into day. Time is always based on change. The change might be the moving hands of a clock or it might be the path of the Sun across the sky, but something must change in order for time to be measured. Since physics tends to deal with objects or situations that change, time is highly important to physicists. This chapter examines how people measure time, the nature of time in physics and in the universe, and whether people will ever be able to travel in time (besides the normal way of just letting time pass).

Another topic of this chapter is the relationship between time and thermodynamics. Although the second law of thermodynamics has a lot to say about time, time was not the primary reason why scientists came up with this law. As discussed in chapter 3, the second law of thermodynamics appeared when people began studying heat engines such as the steam engine. The amazing thing is that out of the study of a simple steam engine came one of the most far-reaching concepts in the universe.

Clocks

Before the physics of time can be investigated, there must be some way of measuring it. The measurement of time is important in almost all branches of physics because many of the equations physicists use involve time. A famous law of motion called Newton's second law, for example, states that the force an object experiences is equal to the product of the object's mass and its acceleration. Time is critical in acceleration, because acceleration is the change in velocity over time. (Velocity also depends on time, since it is equal to the distance traveled per unit time.)

The earliest methods of measuring time were crude but effective for most purposes. All that a person needs to measure time is a periodic event—something that changes at a constant rate. The first events that people used are obvious ones, such as the rising and setting of the Sun or the phases of the Moon. Since the Sun's daily movement governed most people's activities in ancient civilizations, it made sense that the Sun was their timekeeper. The phases of the Moon were used to mark longer periods of time that were roughly the length of months.

Knowing the time of year was critical for ancient peoples. The basis of their economy was farming, and to maximize their crops, they needed some way of telling the best time to plant and to harvest. They also needed to prepare for crucial annual events such as the start of the rainy season or the onset of cold weather. Because a lot of work was involved, they needed to know these things in advance so that they could start in time to finish—it would not do to wait until the frosts came before harvesting.

So many crucial events depended on time that all ancient civilizations developed some sort of calendar. The ancient Egyptians had some of the best timekeeping skills, marking time with a 365-day calendar and a 24-hour day with which most people today are familiar.

But there was a serious problem in all of the calendars used by early peoples. The movement of Earth in its orbit around the Sun governs the seasons and the year—one year corresponds with one complete revolution of the Earth about the Sun, and one day corresponds to one rotation of the planet about its axis. There is no reason that a year must consist of a whole number of days, and it does not. Earth spins on its axis approximately 365 and ¼ times a year, which means there are approximately 365.25 days. The .25 presents a difficulty—using a calendar of a 365 days means that a day will be lost every four years. Although that does not seem like a lot, these lost days add up, and the calendar quickly becomes useless.

The Romans corrected this by the leap year—February of every fourth year had an extra day. This would have worked perfectly if a year was exactly 365.25 days. But more precise measurements indicate that a year is closer to 365.242 days, so once again the calendar gradually became out of step with the seasons. It took hundreds of years for this to happen, but having an average of 365.25 days a year instead of 365.242 finally caught up to people. The situation became so bad that most of Europe switched to a new calendar in the 16th century. This calendar, the Gregorian calendar (named after Pope Gregory, who instituted it), is the one that many people use today. In order to keep the calendar correct over a long period of time, every so often a leap year is skipped. For example, although the year 2000 was a leap year, 1800 and 1900 were not, and the year 2100 will not be a leap year either.

Marking time by days is useful, but there is also a need for measuring shorter intervals. The Sun's motion across the sky provides a crude estimate of the time of day, since in the morning the Sun is near the eastern horizon, at noon it is high overhead, and in the evening it is in the west. To get a more precise measurement of the time of day and to break the day into units of time such as hours, ancient civilizations measured shadows. A sundial consists of a flat plate with a rod or pointer sticking up to make a shadow. The shadow falls on the plate at certain points depending on the Sun's location in the sky, and the approximate time of day can be read. In this way, the day can be divided into intervals. But the problem is that the length of day depends on the season, and the trajectory of the Sun across the sky varies over the course of the year. Reading a sundial depends on knowing the time of year, and even then the measurement is not precise.

For these reasons, people developed other simple devices to measure short periods of time. Sand clocks and water clocks were popular, and both of these clocks measured time by the falling of a substance through a narrow opening. A sand clock marked time by the fall of grains of sand through a container such as an hourglass. A water clock, in its simplest form, is a filled bowl having a small hole near the bottom. The water slowly dripped out, and markings on the bowl indicated the elapsed time as the water level fell. Both of these methods were effective but limited in accuracy. They could also be distorted by crafty people. Some attorneys used bowls with muddy water to time their speeches in court; the mud clogged the hole and the water dripped more slowly, giving these attorneys more time than their rivals to make their case.

As physics became increasingly precise in the 15th and 16th centuries, better timekeepers were necessary. Mechanical devices that performed some kind of periodic motion at a precisely constant rate would do the job, but precision was difficult to achieve. A falling weight might make a good clock because it falls at a constant rate, but it is not periodic and the motion is not naturally broken into small intervals. But eventually people figured out how to use a falling weight in the first clocks. They did this by developing a device that permitted the weight to fall only at very small steps—the ticks of a clock.

Early clocks were made with parts called a foliot and verge, as shown in the figure on page 105. The verge was a rod that could spin and had teeth that fit into a wheel, which when engaged would stop the wheel's movement. The wheel had an attached weight that would cause the wheel to turn except when the verge stopped its movement. The idea of these clocks was that the verge would mark time by letting the weight drop by small distances. To do this, the verge had to let go of the wheel with a periodic motion, and this was the job of the foliot, which was a bar attached to the verge. The foliot moved back and forth, and with each swing, it caused the verge to release the wheel for an instant.

These clocks could divide the time into hours with fairly good accuracy. But the swing of the foliot was not constant—some swings took more time, some swings less—and so the clock could

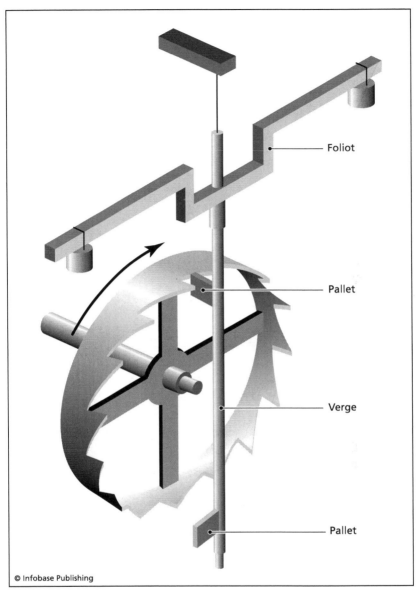

Foliot

Pallet

Verge

Pallet

© Infobase Publishing

A foliot and verge mechanism, called an escapement, is periodic. The foliot swings back and forth, rotating the verge through an angle. On the verge are two extensions called pallets. At the end point of each swing, one of the pallets engages the wheel's teeth and stops its motion. The wheel may have a weight attached or some other mechanism that keeps it turning except when engaged by a pallet, and the job of the foliot and verge is to break the motion into a series of equal steps—the ticks of a clock.

Pendulums and Periodicity

Physicists in the 16th and early 17th centuries had no clocks to measure seconds, so they used what was available. Many used their pulse. But an exciting experiment would cause their heart rate to go up and ruin the measurement!

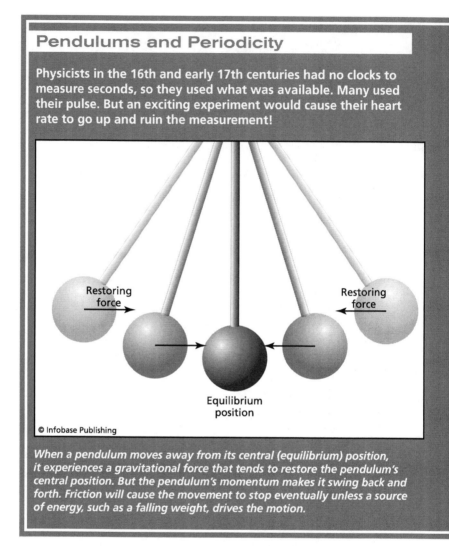

© Infobase Publishing

When a pendulum moves away from its central (equilibrium) position, it experiences a gravitational force that tends to restore the pendulum's central position. But the pendulum's momentum makes it swing back and forth. Friction will cause the movement to stop eventually unless a source of energy, such as a falling weight, drives the motion.

not measure even smaller units of time with enough precision. Clocks that were accurate enough to measure time in seconds could only be made after Galileo (1564–1642) discovered the physics of the pendulum. As discussed in the sidebar on this page, the pendulum is important because in most situations its swing has a rate that is nearly constant and depends only on the pendulum's length. This precise "ticking" can be the basis of an accurate clock.

Galileo realized that the swing of a pendulum makes a good oscillator. A pendulum is a bar or a weight attached to a string that is connected to a pivot point at the top, as shown in the figure on page 106. When the pendulum is not moving, it hangs straight down, but a little push makes the pendulum swing—the force of gravity causes it to fall back and forth. The farthest that the pendulum reaches during its swing is called the amplitude. The period is the time required for the pendulum to make one full swing. The period is important because clocks can only be accurate if their ticking involves oscillatory (back-and-forth) motion with an unvarying period. *Frequency* is another term used to describe an oscillation, and it equals the number of back-and-forth cycles per second. The unit of frequency is the *Hertz*, which is one cycle per second. (The Hertz is named after Heinrich Hertz [1857–94], a German physicist who studied electromagnetic radiation and its frequencies.) Frequency is the inverse of period, so an oscillation having a period of 0.25 seconds has a frequency of 1/(0.25) = four cycles per second.

Pendulums make good clocks because they have regular, constant periods. At small amplitudes, the period depends on the length of the pendulum but not on the amplitude. (At higher amplitudes, this is not true, which is undesirable because it can cause the period to vary.) Although Galileo put a lot of thought into the mechanism of pendulum clocks, the first one was built by Dutch physicist Christiaan Huygens (1629–95) in 1656.

Pendulum clocks need something to give the pendulum a little boost (such as a falling weight in many "grandfather" clocks that use pendulums), otherwise the swing would gradually stop due to friction. Clockmakers also have to worry about thermal expansion; the period of a pendulum depends on its length, and if the period varies, so does the clock. Pendulums in the most accurate clocks are often made of material that does not expand much with temperature.

The pendulum solved many of the problems of time measurement. With pendulum clocks, physicists could conduct accurate experiments, and people could know exactly what time of the day it was. When a church or school met at 9:00 in the morning, there was no excuse for being late.

There was one problem, however, that pendulum clocks could not solve. This problem was important because it affected commerce, the development of trade, and the exploration of the world.

The weight of the three cylinders in this grandfather clock provide the force to keep the pendulum swinging. *(Kyle Kirkland)*

The problem pendulums could not solve involved the measurement of a ship's location at sea. What sailors needed was an accurate clock that worked on the shifting, rolling deck of a ship—a place where the motion was too severe for pendulum clocks to function well.

Why was time needed to determine a ship's location? Any spot on the surface of Earth can be identified by its latitude—the north-south distance from the equator—and its longitude, the location along the east-west direction. Latitude was not a problem, at least in the Northern Hemisphere, because navigators could use the North Star, whose height above the horizon varies with latitude. Longitude was the reason why time became involved.

Longitude can be determined by using the position of the stars, but the problem is that stars except the North Star move during the night. (The North Star, *Polaris,* is almost directly above Earth's axis of rotation—the North Pole—so the planet's spin does not change this star's position in the sky.) To find longitude from the stars, navigators needed to not only measure the position of the stars but also know the time of night they were making the measurement. Just knowing the day of the year was not good enough, the exact time mattered. This required an accurate clock.

The problem was severe enough that in 1714 England's government offered a reward of £20,000 to anyone who could make a clock accurate enough to permit longitude measurement. (Today this amount of money in American currency would be worth more than a million dollars.) The money inspired a huge number of attempts, all of which failed in some way or another, but finally a carpenter and clockmaker named John Harrison succeeded. A new and improved set of timekeeping pieces resulted.

The clocks of Harrison and the clockmakers that followed him were based on either springs or wheels. These items had been used earlier, but Harrison had to make adjustments in order to increase their accuracy. Wheels, and the foliots mentioned earlier, fail to be perfectly periodic. Springs can be used to run a clock—somewhat like a falling weight—but the force exerted by a spring varies depending on its compression. These are the problems that Harrison and others had to solve. They did so with elaborate and complex mechanisms, all of which ensured that the ticks of the clock were precisely equal, or, in other words, that the clock's motion was steady and periodic.

Springs became common in small clocks such as wristwatches, but today clocks and watches that need to be wound (in order to compress the spring) are much less popular. Oscillations used to drive clocks include alternating current electricity, which in the United States oscillates at 60 cycles per second, and the vibration of an instrument called a tuning fork. Musicians use tuning forks to tune their instruments because tuning forks oscillate at a precise frequency. This precise frequency is also what makes tuning forks useful to timekeepers, since the periodic motion is an excellent basis for a clock.

In the 1950s, electric watches began to appear, run by batteries. Today many wristwatches have a quartz crystal (a material found in white sand) that oscillates at a precise frequency when it is controlled with electricity. The best quartz crystal clocks are accurate to within a few milliseconds (thousandths of a second) per year.

Physicists of the 20th century began experimenting with tiny pieces of matter and found even better oscillators—atoms. Atoms emit energy in the form of electromagnetic radiation at remarkably precise frequencies. Light is electromagnetic radiation of a certain frequency (in the range of 425,000,000,000–750,000,000,000 Hertz), but electromagnetic radiation exists at a lot of different frequencies (radio waves, microwaves, and X-rays are other examples of electromagnetic radiation). The radiation emitted under certain circumstances by cesium atoms is quite stable and has been used as the basis of "atomic" clocks, which can be accurate to within a few milliseconds per 1,000 years. Atoms are useful in clocks not only because of their precise periodicity but also because they are not affected by mechanical and thermal disturbances that disrupt pendulums, crystals, and springs. The radiation of the cesium atom is so precise that in 1967 scientists used it to define the second—a second is officially the duration of 9,192,631,770 oscillations of the cesium atom.

Time and the Laws of Physics

Physicists know the time with amazing accuracy, which allows them to make precise measurements, but do they really understand time itself? Several physicists of the 20th century did not think so. One of the most important of these physicists was Albert Einstein (1879–1955).

What bothered Einstein was the concept of absolute time—that there was a single time that was correct for everyone in the universe. Einstein believed that time was relative to the observer. One of the reasons for his belief was that he assumed—correctly, as it turned out—that the speed of light is the same for all observers. Time is related to light because observers see events by the light reaching their eyes, and the speed that light travels to reach the eyes will affect the time at which the observer sees an event; in order to detect that something happened at a point in space, light from the event must travel from that point to an observer's eyes. Einstein believed that if light behaved the way he thought it did, then the time at which two observers see the same event can be different. If the speed of light is constant for all observers, Einstein realized that two observers may be moving at different speeds and therefore light may not reach them at the same instant. This would cause them to disagree on what time the event occurred.

Einstein's ideas initially did not make any sense to other physicists, because they believed the opposite was true: time was the same for all observers (absolute time) and the speed of light was relative. They believed the speed of light was relative because it should depend on the speed of the object emitting the light. Consider, for instance, a person who is walking at three miles per hour (4.8 km/hr.) and steps on a conveyor belt that is moving at four miles per hour (6.4 km/hr.). If the person continues to walk at the same pace, then the person's speed on the conveyor (as measured by someone standing still) is $3 + 4 = 7$ miles per hour (11.2 km/hr.). (Although the physics of the situation is more complex than this, for slow speeds a simple addition is often accurate enough.) Physicists thought the same should happen to light—if the speed of light emitted from a stationary car headlight is c, then the speed of light coming from the headlight of a car moving at 60 miles per hour (96 km/hr.) is $c + 60$ (or, using kilometers, $c + 96$). But this is false. Einstein was correct—the speed of light is the same regardless of the velocity of the emitting object. The speed of light in a vacuum is 186,200 miles per second (300,000 km/s), and it will always travel at this rate regardless of the velocity of the source. (Light's speed does depend on the substance through which it travels—the speed of light in water, for example, is about 25 percent slower than it is in empty space).

Einstein first published his ideas on time and the speed of light in 1905, and the theory became known as the special theory of relativity. One of the strangest consequences of this theory is time dilation. Time is relative to the observer, and Einstein proposed that time is dilated—slowed down—for people who are traveling at high speeds. This means time moves more slowly for an astronaut riding on a fast spaceship than a person staying on Earth. Although it sounds unbelievable, physicists have done experiments to support this idea. For example, by using extremely accurate atomic clocks, physicists have shown that time actually slows down when the clock is moving at high speed. The effect is tiny unless the speed is close to the speed of light, and since no one has built a vehicle that goes anywhere near that fast, for most speeds with which people are familiar here on Earth time dilation is too small to worry about. But the effect is real, and Einstein's theory appears to be correct.

The theories of Einstein caused people to think carefully about the nature of time. But there is another relation between time and the laws of physics that is just as important—the direction in which time seems to "flow."

Nearly all of the laws and equations physicists use do not indicate a direction for time. The equations work fine whether time is moving forward or backward. What this means mathematically is that in these equations there is a variable t, which stands for time, and the equation is correct whether t is getting larger (the normal direction of time, where time is "flowing" forward) or t is getting smaller (the opposite direction, where time is going backward).

Consider a scene from a movie. A viewer normally watches the movie in the forward direction, but if the movie is on tape or DVD, then it can be watched in reverse. Familiar events happen in the forward direction—for example, a car crashes into a wall, and the car's front end crumples. The movie looks funny in the reverse direction, as the car's crumpled front end suddenly straightens itself out and the car takes off in reverse. This is such an unlikely event that viewers can tell the movie is not going in the "right" direction.

But the equations of physics seem to be fine whether they are going forward or backward in time. The movement of the planets, which is governed by gravitation, is a good example. If a distant observer watching the Sun's solar system made a movie of Earth and the other planets moving around the Sun, the movie would like realistic even if it was played in reverse. If from the viewer's perspective, the planets move in a clockwise motion in their orbits, then when the movie is played in reverse the planets would move in the opposite direction, counterclockwise, but there is nothing

Car crashes, such as this relatively minor one, provide a direction for the flow of time—viewers never see the reverse of a crash, where a damaged vehicle straightens itself out. *(Kyle Kirkland)*

wrong with that. Planets can move in either direction, and there are surely examples of both among the many solar systems of the galaxy.

Electromagnetism provides another example. A generator produces electricity from the motion of an electric conductor in a magnetic field, and an electric motor produces motion by using a changing magnetic field to push an electric conductor. The two processes are the reverse of each other—an electric motor is an electric generator run in reverse. (According to one story, the first people to discover electric motors did so because they accidentally wired an electric generator backward!)

But there is an exception in which physics has a single direction in time. Rubber objects fall down and bounce up, yet a movie of a bouncing ball would not be the same in the forward direction as in the reverse, because a bouncing ball gradually loses height and finally stops bouncing. In reverse, the movie would show a ball resting on the floor that suddenly begins to bounce. Although this effect might seem to have something to do with gravity, it does not. What is important here is thermodynamics and a concept called *entropy*.

Entropy and Disorder

Entropy is a measure of order and organization (or disorder and disorganization, depending on one's viewpoint). The reason physicists started thinking about order is Carnot's theory. As discussed in chapter 3, Carnot correctly realized that no heat engine could ever be 100 percent efficient. Efficiency determines the amount of work a machine does for a given amount of heat input, and what Carnot said was that some of the heat's energy will always be wasted. The wasted heat does no work, it simply escapes in the heat engine's exhaust. This theory applies to all heat engines, from the steam engines of Carnot's day to the jet engines of today.

Carnot's theory puzzled physicists, and out of their curiosity came the concept of entropy. The beauty of this idea is that it explains a lot more than just the odd behavior of heat engines.

To understand entropy, one must understand the notion of order and disorder. Consider a pack of cards. Suppose the cards are in order, running from low to high, and the suits (spades, hearts, diamonds, and clubs) are also neatly arranged. But then someone throws the cards up in the air, and they scatter everywhere. If the cards are picked up at random, their sequence will almost certainly be out of order. Now suppose someone throws the out-of-order cards into the air and the cards are picked up at random, as before. Will the new arrangement of cards return to the proper order? Once again, this is highly unlikely; the sequence of cards will be different than before, but they will not be in order, they will have a different out-of-order arrangement.

Everyone is familiar with processes similar to the card experiment described above. All things tend to get more disorganized and disordered over time—machines break down; carefully stacked piles topple over; fresh and clean objects get dirty and erode, rust, or simply wear down. The opposite does not tend to happen, at least not without help—disordered or dirty objects do not tend to become ordered and clean without someone doing a lot of work.

The old gravestone on the left has suffered the ravages of time, losing its shape and engraving. The gravestone on the right is newer. *(Kyle Kirkland)*

Another example is the way that an odor spreads throughout a room. If a person wearing perfume walks into a room, initially the odor can only be detected by people who are nearby, but soon the odor molecules travel and fill up the room, and everyone smells it. Once the odor molecules fill the whole room, they stay there—they do not suddenly return to a small space surrounding the perfumed person. (Some of the people in the room might wish this would happen, but it never does.) The odor molecules were at first confined to a small space and so they were initially more organized, but gradually they spread evenly throughout all available space and so the odor molecules became disorganized—just like an orderly pile of sand becomes disorganized when it is shaken and spread across the floor.

Heat is yet another example. When a hot object enters a cold room, gradually the object's temperature falls and the rest of the room warms up a little—the heat spreads throughout the room, whereas the energy was initially confined to the hot object. Because this is true, heat is the basis of one way to measure entropy, which is not surprising since thermodynamics was the primary reason why physicists starting thinking about the concept. The change in entropy, ΔS (the symbol Δ *means "change in"*), of an object or a system is given by the heat, Q, flowing into (or out of) it, divided by the temperature, T (given in the Kelvin scale):

$$\Delta S = Q/T.$$

Measurements show that entropy always increases for a *spontaneous process*—a process that occurs naturally, without any outside help. Heat naturally flows from hot objects to cold, and in the process, entropy increases. An ordered pack of cards becomes random when scattered over the floor. Molecules initially confined in a small corner eventually spread throughout the entire room. Ordered systems have low entropy and disordered systems have high entropy. As time passes, orderly systems became increasingly disordered. No matter what the process, entropy tends to increase. This important statement, discussed in the following sidebar, is one way of stating the second law of thermodynamics.

Entropy explains the mystery of Carnot's theory concerning the efficiency of heat engines. The heat lost in the exhaust is necessary

Second Law of Thermodynamics Revisited

Chapter 3 described the second law of thermodynamics in terms of heat and work. This is perfectly correct, but there is another way of formulating the second law: in an isolated system, entropy will stay the same or increase over time, it will not decrease. In other words, in an object or system that is not influenced by any outside activity, order will tend to turn into disorder.

But if everything tends to get more disorganized over time, how does anything ever get ordered in the first place? What the second law says is that entropy generally increases in isolated systems and for spontaneous processes. A refrigerator pumps heat from the cold interior to the warm room outside, so the interior of the refrigerator gets cooler and, according to the simple equation given above, the entropy inside decreases—the refrigerator removes heat, and the change in heat is therefore negative. But this is not a spontaneous process because the refrigerator had to do work, and it would not function if someone pulled the plug. If the whole system of objects is taken together, then the second law says that the entropy increases—the entropy is reduced inside the refrigerator (because of the work done by electricity), but the refrigerator pumps heat into the room, and the room's entropy increases. In any process, the sum of the entropy of all affected objects either stays the same or, more likely, rises. That is the second law.

There is one more important consideration of the second law of thermodynamics—it is a statistical law, not an absolute one. This means that the law does not guarantee the predicted outcome—a rise in entropy—although it is extremely likely to occur. The reason for this is clear from considering the card experiment discussed earlier. If someone throws an out-of-order pack of cards onto the floor and picks up the cards at random, it is possible, although highly unlikely, that the resulting sequence of cards will be ordered. There is also a small chance that the resulting sequence could be slightly more ordered than before, so that although it is not perfectly ordered it is better than it was before. In this case, entropy would have increased slightly. But because there are so many more states of a system that are disordered than ordered, almost always a system that evolves in time (without any help from the outside) will end up in a more disordered state. The pack of cards, for example, has only one perfectly ordered sequence and a huge number of other possible sequences, many of which are quite jumbled. In systems with more elements than a pack of cards—and most systems have a huge number of elements—an increase in entropy is overwhelmingly probable.

so that the entropy of the whole system (the heat engine and the surroundings) increases, or at the very least, stays the same. Otherwise the heat engine would not work. Some engineers consider the heat lost in the exhaust of heat engines a "fee" or a "tribute" that must be paid to the second law of thermodynamics.

Thermodynamics also explains the failure of a bouncing ball to continue bouncing. The loss of energy is converted into heat— the ball and the object on which it is bouncing both get slightly warmer. Heat is disordered motion, as discussed in chapter 1— heat is the random motion of an object's atoms and molecules. The second law of thermodynamics says that spontaneous processes get more disordered, and this includes motion. The neat, orderly up-and-down motion of the ball slowly gets transformed into random motion of atoms and molecules, and temperature rises. Basketball players must keep bouncing the ball with their hands in order to dribble toward the hoop, otherwise the second law of thermodynamics would leave the ball on the court behind them.

Entropy is what provides physics with a direction of time. The flow of time is in the direction of increasing entropy, or disorder. While watching the movie scene with the car accident, as mentioned earlier, viewers realize something is wrong when the film is run backward and the crumpled car straightens itself out. What is wrong is that the second law makes it extremely unlikely that objects and processes spontaneously go from a disordered state to an ordered one.

Traveling in Time

The second law of thermodynamics, which says that entropy generally increases over time, is what gives time a direction in which to flow. But some people have wondered whether it is possible to travel through time in any direction or any speed they wish.

In a sense, everyone travels in time—slowly and in the forward direction. The question is whether the journey can in some way be altered. The answer is yes, thanks to Einstein's ideas.

As mentioned earlier, Einstein said that time slows down at high speeds. Physicists have tested this idea, and the results support the theory. This means it is possible to get time to slow down by hopping aboard a fast spaceship. The spaceship must be able to travel at a significant fraction of the speed of light or the effect will be too small to notice. Although such speeds are not possible at present, they may become reachable in the future. With such a ship, astronauts could go to places that are so far away it would take hundreds of years to reach them. But the hundreds of years would be "Earth time"—because time slows down for the astronauts, they would not experience this much time, nor would they age for that long. In "ship time," they might spend only a few years. This concept has been the basis of many science fiction stories and movies, such as *Planet of the Apes* (the original movie was released in 1968 and starred Charlton Heston). The astronauts in *Planet of the Apes* make a voyage that to them lasts only a few months, but 2,000 years pass on Earth. The science in this science fiction movie is based on real physics.

Future spacecraft are shown here flying in formation. This drawing depicts a possible mission to locate Earthlike planets orbiting other stars. *(NASA)*

What about traveling in the other direction, into the past? This may not be so easy.

The whole idea seems absurd, at least at first. The past has already occurred and is long gone, so it would seem impossible for anyone to go to a place that no longer exists. But as far as physics is concerned, time is relative. What is past for one person is not necessarily past for the universe as a whole. Maybe traveling into the past is possible, though it is certainly difficult to conceive.

One possible method of traveling backward in time makes use of another one of Einstein's ideas. Einstein said not only does time slow down at high speeds, but it also slows down because of gravity. Once again Einstein was right, because physicists have made measurements with precise atomic clocks and determined that they run slower as gravity increases.

In most situations, time's interaction with gravity is not significant. But in one case, involving strange and mysterious objects, there are some interesting possibilities. One of these objects is called a black hole. Physicists believe black holes form when matter becomes so dense that the force of gravitation squeezes it down into a point called a singularity. Matter is normally strong enough to withstand gravitational forces, except when a large amount of matter, such as the amount of matter in a large star (much bigger than the Sun), is compressed into a small space. While the star is shining, there are energetic reactions taking place inside to generate enough force to prevent the star's matter from getting pulled inward due to gravitation. But when the reactions stop—and they will, for all stars shine from energy released in nuclear reactions but eventually run out of fuel—gravitational forces cause the star to collapse. The star gets denser, which increases the force of gravitation. Soon gravitation becomes too strong for matter to withstand it. The physics of what happens next is not entirely clear, but apparently the matter gets squeezed into a point of practically infinite density.

Black holes get their name because their gravity is strong enough to prevent light from escaping (and so they appear totally black). They are "holes" because they are places where a star was once located but now is gone. Black holes cannot be seen, but they can be detected because their gravitational force remains.

Astronomers believe they have found several objects in the galaxy that may be black holes, including one in the center of the galaxy with a mass a million times greater than the Sun.

Gravity is so strong near a black hole's singularity that time appears to come to a halt to any outside observers. In the singularity itself, time does not really have any well-understood meaning (nor do any of the other basic concepts in physics). But some physicists believe under certain circumstances singularities may provide a tunnel to other places—and perhaps other times. These ideas are speculative, meaning they have not been confirmed by experiment. The physics is extremely complicated, and no one knows for sure what is happening inside a black hole, and more to the point, no one knows how to survive the journey to find out. Gravitational forces would be so strong that except under special circumstances they would tear apart anyone who tried.

Another possible backward time-travel method involves an object called a wormhole (also known as an Einstein-Rosen bridge). A wormhole is a tunnel through space and time. No one knows if wormholes exist, but some of Einstein's theories seem to allow the possibility. In theory, wormholes are caused by the presence of large masses such as black holes, and the idea is that these masses link together, forming a bridge. The bridge would be like a shortcut, and a traveler could pass quickly through vast distances and, perhaps, time as well.

Although some physicists believe backward time travel may be possible, there are more concerns than just physics. Traveling backward in time can create a paradox—an impossible situation. For instance, in the 1985 movie *Back to the Future*, a young man goes back in time hoping to meet his parents when they were his age. But the young man finds himself in trouble when he nearly becomes responsible for preventing his parents from falling in love with each other—which would have disastrous consequences for him, their future son!

The paradoxes created by traveling backward in time, such as a person preventing his or her own birth, suggests these journeys are not possible. It is difficult to understand how a time traveler could make a change that affects the future. Even more difficult is how time travelers could affect their own future to the extent of preventing themselves from ever existing!

Perhaps time travel into the past is impossible after all. This would explain the absence of any known visitors from the future—if backward time travel becomes possible in the future, one would think there would be people dropping in from the future, since the present time—today, for example—is their past. At present there is no well-understood law of physics that precludes backward time travel, and some serious thought, as mentioned above, has gone into considering the possibility. Yet the potential paradoxes indicate there is probably a law of physics to prevent such travel. If so, finding this law is important because it may reveal much more than is presently known about the nature of time.

The Beginning and the End of the Universe

A complete understanding of time would have to include the whole history of the universe. Most people who lived prior to the 20th century believed their universe had no beginning or ending, and if this were true, the same could be said about time. Time would be infinite, lasting forever.

But today most physicists believe the universe began about 14 billion years ago. The big bang theory suggests that the universe began as a singularity—an infinitely dense point—and expanded to its present size. There are several reasons why this theory is widely accepted. Careful measurements by astronomers show that the galaxies are moving apart, with a speed that increases with distance—distant galaxies are moving at high speeds, in some cases a considerable fraction of the speed of light. This movement occurs despite gravitational attraction, which is always at work. (The force of gravitation is strong enough to cause the closest galaxies to move together, but in general the galaxies of the universe are moving away from each other.) The universe is expanding, and physicists account for this by saying that space itself is expanding. Other astronomical measurements also support the big bang theory—for instance, energy called cosmic background radiation is believed to be leftover energy from the creation of the universe.

If the universe had a beginning, how did it get its start? This is one of the basic questions of a branch of science called cosmology (the term *cosmos* comes from a Greek word referring to the universe). The physics is complicated, and while scientists have proposed theories to explain many of the early events of the universe—such as how the forces of nature arose and why matter formed the stars and galaxies—the laws of physics, at least as they are currently understood, do not permit a mathematical description of the earliest moments of the universe. At a time of about 10^{-35} seconds and earlier, the universe was so hot and dense that its description is beyond the present reach of physics. The 10^{-35} seconds is an unimaginably tiny period of time, but, nevertheless, it means a complete understanding of the beginning of the universe—and of time—is not yet possible.

Some people are uncomfortable with the notion of a beginning for time. If time began at the big bang, what came before? Perhaps this question has no meaning, or at least no meaning in terms of physics. Although people can ask, and wonder, about this question, it may have no answer. Everything that people experience or can imagine experiencing has a beginning, so the question is a natural one, but the beginning of the universe is an event well beyond the range of human experience—and perhaps understanding as well. On the other hand, science proceeds by asking questions, and no one knows for sure whether this question has an answer or not.

Much of the universe is still a mystery, but the second law of thermodynamics has something to say about its evolution over time. The entropy of an isolated system increases, and the universe is certainly an isolated system—the universe is all that exists, so nothing from the outside should be able to influence it. According to the second law, the entropy of the universe is increasing. The universe is becoming more and more disordered as time goes by.

If time and the universe had a beginning, it is possible they have an ending as well. What kind of ending will eventually occur depends on whether the universe continues to expand or not. The big bang sent the universe flying out in every direction, but matter also experiences an attractive force due to gravitation. If the density of the universe is large enough, gravitation will win, and the expansion will come to a halt. If not, the expansion will probably continue forever. Measurements of the amount of matter in the universe and measurements of the present expansion rate are difficult to make and sometimes present conflicting evidence, but at the present time, the best guess is that the universe will continue to expand. Recent measurements indicate that the expansion is even accelerating, perhaps by the presence of some kind of "dark energy" that propels matter further apart.

As the expansion goes on, entropy will continue to increase. This gives rise to one possible fate of the universe—"heat death." Entropy rises to a maximum, and at this point, the universe becomes totally disordered. As discussed in the last chapter, the second law of thermodynamics requires heat engines to discard some heat in the engine's exhaust so that entropy increases, otherwise the engine cannot do any work. When entropy reaches a maximum, this will not be possible and, according to the second law of thermodynamics, there can be no more work from heat engines.

If the universe continues expanding, then the notion of time, if not time itself, would probably have an end. Time always involves change—some sort of regular, periodic change, whether it is the rotation of the Earth, the swing of a pendulum, or the oscillation of an atom's radiation. When the universe gets old enough for entropy to rise to a maximum, there will be few orderly changes, so time would be difficult or impossible to measure. But there is no cause for concern at present—time has billions of years more to go before all is said and done.

CONCLUSION

THERMODYNAMIC PRINCIPLES EMBODIED by the second law and Carnot's engine will always limit the efficiency of heat engines, regardless of their operation and composition. But often these limits have not yet been reached, as is the case with automobile engines, and there is still room for improvement. Although the laws of thermodynamics demand that some heat be discarded in the exhaust, a lot of heat also needlessly escapes from today's engines and raises the temperature of the surrounding material. Further study of heat transfer in various substances and materials may lead to better insulators and improved methods of retaining this heat, allowing it to do work instead of simply heating up a car's hood or a jet engine casing.

Thermodynamics research also holds promise in other endeavors, many of which involve practical engineering problems—the kind of problem that motivated the study of thermodynamics in the first place. But some of this research strikes a more fundamental chord. One of the most interesting research programs involves the origin of life.

The question of life's beginnings is controversial because for many people it is not just a question of science but also involves important religious beliefs. Science may or may not have anything to say about religion—this is also a controversial question—but most scientists today believe Earth formed about 4.5 billion years ago and life arose when large molecules combined and began to replicate themselves. Paleontologists (scientists who study ancient life-forms) are unsure exactly when life arose—the oldest indication of life is in rocks 3.5 billion years old, but such remains are tiny, and some scientists are not certain whether these remains are really fossils of living organisms or were formed by some chemical process unrelated to life. But fossils clearly show up in 2.5-billion-year-old rocks, so life must have began billions of years ago.

If life evolved when molecules combined together and began to replicate—and assuming that no one was present to guide the process—then life sprang from self-organization. Life is an organized and orderly arrangement of matter, so in the beginning, matter escaped its normal state—disorder—and transformed itself into a complex and orderly unit. Thermodynamics and the concept of entropy are critical in this kind of process.

Self-organization might seem impossible—it would be like a city forming itself out of a forest or a house assembling itself from raw materials. Order decreases entropy, which is highly unlikely for a spontaneous process, especially a large and complex process such as a house, a city, or even a tiny single-celled organism. But only in isolated systems is entropy overwhelmingly likely to rise. Entropy and the second law of thermodynamics do not rule out orderly arrangements; these concepts merely suggest that some input of energy is necessary. Self-organization can occur if there is an external source of energy to drive the process and, taking into account the whole system—the energy source along with life's starting materials—entropy rose. This is similar to a heat engine, which can do work and cause a local decrease in entropy as long as the process exhausts some heat into the environment so that the overall entropy will rise.

The energy source that sparked early life is not known. In 1953, American chemist Harold Urey and his student Stanley Miller performed an experiment with a sterilized flask of ammonia, methane, water, and hydrogen, which they believed was similar to conditions on Earth billions of years ago. For an energy source they used sparks of electricity mimicking lightning. Urey and Miller opened the flasks in a few days and discovered complex molecules associated with life, such as amino acids. This was one of the earliest experiments showing the formation of complex molecules from simple components.

Thermodynamics involves entropy, time, energy conversion and transfer, and is a fundamental consideration in the study and search for the origin of life. The apparent impossibility of backward time travel means that no one will probably ever be able to observe what really happened, so scientists must use the concepts and theories of thermodynamics, along with fossils and the principles of biology, to piece the story together.

At the present time, the origin of life is filled with mysteries. Because of experiments like those of Urey and Miller, the formation of complex organic molecules—the building blocks of life—is not difficult to understand. But no one knows how these molecules organized themselves into living cells. Cells have complex arrangements of genes made out of DNA, proteins made from amino acids that perform many vital tasks, and a highly complex metabolism to convert energy in the form of food into fuel to operate life's many tasks (a process that decreases entropy in the organism but increases entropy in the environment). How life arose from complex molecules is a scientific problem whose possible solutions will be informed, and constrained, by the laws of thermodynamics.

SI Units and Conversions

Unit	Quantity	Symbol	Conversion
Base Units			
meter	length	m	1 m = 3.28 feet
kilogram	mass	kg	
second	time	s	
ampere	electric current	A	
Kelvin	thermodynamic temperature	K	1 K = 1°C = 1.8°F
candela	luminous intensity	cd	
mole	amount of substance	mol	
Supplementary Units			
radian	plane angle	rad	π rad = 180 degrees
Derived Units (combinations of base or supplementary units)			
Coulomb	electric charge	C	
cubic meter	volume	m^3	1 m^3 = 1,000 liters = 264 gallons
farad	capacitance	F	
Henry	inductance	H	

Unit	Quantity	Symbol	Conversion
Derived Units (continued)			
Hertz	frequency	Hz	1 Hz = 1 cycle per second
meter/second	speed	m/s	1 m/s = 2.24 miles/hour
Newton	force	N	4.4482 N = 1 pound
Ohm	electric resistance	Ω	
Pascal	pressure	Pa	101,325 Pa = 1 atmosphere
radian/second	angular speed	rad/s	π rad/s = 180 degrees/second
Tesla	magnetic flux density	T	
volt	electromotive force	V	
Watt	power	W	746 W = 1 horsepower

UNIT PREFIXES

Prefixes alter the value of the unit.

Example: kilometer = 10^3 meters (1,000 meters)

Prefix	Multiplier	Symbol
femto	10^{-15}	f
pico	10^{-12}	p
nano	10^{-9}	n
micro	10^{-6}	μ
milli	10^{-3}	m
centi	10^{-2}	c
deci	10^{-1}	d
deca	10	da
hecto	10^2	h
kilo	10^3	k
mega	10^6	M
giga	10^9	G
tera	10^{12}	T

GLOSSARY

absolute scale   a temperature scale based on a unit called Kelvin (K) that has the same magnitude as the Celsius degree; the scale assigns the number 0 to absolute zero

absolute zero temperature   the lowest possible temperature, equal to $-459.69°F$ ($-273.15°C$) and designated as 0 K in the absolute temperature scale

albedo   the percentage of light hitting a surface that is reflected

body temperature   in warm-blooded animals, the relatively constant temperature of the body, such as the human body temperature that averages about $98.2°F$ ($36.8°C$)

Carnot engine   an ideal heat engine having the best possible efficiency

conduction   the transfer of heat through a substance

conductor   a material that readily permits heat flow, or conduction

conformation   the three-dimensional shape of a molecule

convection   the transfer of heat by the movement of a fluid

displacement   in internal combustion engines, the amount of volume the pistons displace (move through), which is a measure of their ability to do work

ectothermy   obtaining heat from the environment, as in "cold-blooded" animals

endothermy   the ability to generate heat, as in "warm-blooded" animals

energy   the ability to do work

entropy   a measure of a system's organization (the amount of disorder of a system)

enzyme a molecule, usually a protein, that speeds up a chemical reaction without being consumed or changed by the reaction

fever a prolonged elevation of body temperature, usually caused by infection

first law of thermodynamics the change in energy of a system equals the net amount of work performed and the net heat flow; this law is a statement of the principle of energy conservation, which says that energy is neither created nor destroyed

fluid air or liquid, which are often classed together as fluids because their properties are similar

frequency the number of cycles per second (Hertz) of a periodic event or waveform

friction a resistance to motion caused by the contact or rubbing of two or more objects

greenhouse effect a rise in temperature caused by the absorption of infrared radiation by atmospheric gases such as carbon dioxide, water vapor, and chlorofluorocarbons

heat energy that flows between objects having different temperatures

heat capacity the amount of heat necessary to raise the temperature of a body by one degree

heat engine a machine that converts thermal energy into work

heat transfer the transmission of heat between objects, accomplished by the mechanisms of conduction, convection, or radiation

Hertz unit of frequency, equal to one cycle per second

horsepower a measure of power, originally defined as the raising of 550 pounds by one foot in one second (roughly the rate of work of a single horse), and equal to about 746 watts in the metric system units

hypothermia a dangerous decrease in body temperature

infrared radiation invisible electromagnetic radiation having a frequency slightly lower than visible light

internal combustion engine heat engine in which the fuel burns (combusts) in a compartment or chamber located within, or internal to the engine, such as in a cylinder

jet engine   heat engine that creates forward thrust by expelling liquids or gases out from a rear nozzle

Kelvin   *see* ABSOLUTE SCALE

kinetic energy   the energy of motion

latent heat   the amount of energy required to change a substance's phase at the transition temperature

pendulum   an early clock that relied on the regular oscillation of a swinging mass

phase   state of matter (gas, liquid, solid, or plasma)

power   the rate at which energy is used or produced

protein   a large biological molecule that folds up into a specific conformation and performs a specific function, such as an enzyme speeding up a chemical reaction

radiation   transfer of energy through space via electromagnetic waves

reactant   one of the substances participating in a chemical reaction

rpm   revolutions per minute

second law of thermodynamics   it is impossible for a machine to convert all the heat, drawn from some body or object at a given temperature, into work; an alternative formulation, in terms of entropy, is that the entropy of an isolated system rises

spontaneous process   an event or process that happens naturally, without any help or stimulation

state   the condition, arrangement, or phase of a system

steam engine   heat engine that uses steam as the source of energy

supercharger   a compressor designed to get more oxygen into an engine's piston cylinder by squeezing the air into a small space, in order to boost the amount of combustion

temperature   a measure of the hotness or coldness of an object, corresponding to the amount of internal motion of its atoms and molecules

thermal energy   energy of a body arising from the energies of its atoms and molecules, which flows between objects having different temperatures

thermal equilibrium   the state of a system at which there is no heat flow because all the objects are at the same temperature

thermal expansion   the increase in volume of an object when its temperature increases

thermal insulator   a material that is a poor conductor of heat

thermodynamics   the study of heat and its relation to other forms of energy

thermography   a measurement of the distribution of temperature of an object or body

thermometer   a device to measure temperature

thermophile   an organism that thrives in hot environments

third law of thermodynamics   an object can never be cooled to absolute zero

turbine   a machine that rotates under the force of an expanding gas or liquid

turbocharger   a compressor, powered by an engine's exhaust, that increases the oxygen in the fuel chamber and therefore increases the amount of combustion

work   the amount of energy expended to cause an object's motion, calculated by multiplying the amount of force that caused the motion by the distance the object moves

zeroth law of thermodynamics   when heat can flow between objects, the objects will eventually stabilize at the same temperature (thermal equilibrium)

FURTHER READING AND WEB SITES

BOOKS

Atkins, P. W. *The Second Law.* New York: W. H. Freeman & Company, 1984. Written by a scientist, this book examines the second law of thermodynamics from a conceptual, nonmathematical perspective.

Bloomfield, Louis A. *How Things Work: The Physics of Everyday Life.* 3rd ed. New York: Wiley, 2005. This is a college-level text but is easy to understand and covers a wide range of phenomena.

Calle, Carlos I. *Superstrings and Other Things: A Guide to Physics.* Bristol: Institute of Physics, 2001. Calle explains the laws and principles of physics in a clear and accessible manner.

Davies, Paul. *How to Build a Time Machine.* New York: Penguin, 2003. Focusing on black holes and wormholes, this book describes what a scientifically plausible time machine could look like and how it might work.

Hawking, Stephen. *The Universe in a Nutshell.* New York: Bantam, 2001. Hawking, a physicist well known for his work involving gravitation and cosmology, presents a fascinating tour of the universe in this richly illustrated volume.

Goldstein, Martin, and Inge F. Goldstein. *The Refrigerator and the Universe: Understanding the Laws of Energy.* Cambridge, Mass.: Harvard University Press, 1995. Accessible reading material on thermodynamics is rare, but this book explains the laws and concepts of thermodynamics on a basic and enjoyable level.

Kras, Sara Louise. *The Steam Engine.* Philadelphia: Chelsea House Publishers, 2004. Not only does this book describe the development of this revolutionary device, but it also discusses how and why the steam machine changed society, industry, and economy.

Pickover, Clifford A. *Time: A Traveler's Guide.* Oxford: Oxford University Press, 1999. A noted science writer, Pickover offers a lighthearted but scientifically accurate look at time and time travel.

Smil, Vaclav. *Energies.* Cambridge, Mass.: MIT Press, 1999. A look at energy and how its many forms shape and contribute to civilization and the environment.

Suplee, Curt. *The New Everyday Science Explained.* Washington, D.C.: National Geographic Society, 2004. Concise scientific answers to some of the most basic questions about people and nature. Richly illustrated.

Von Baeyer, Hans Christian. *Warmth Disperses and Time Passes: The History of Heat.* New York: Modern Library, 1999. This volume explores the evolution of the science of thermodynamics, providing insight into how the laws of thermodynamics were discovered and what they mean.

WEB SITES

American Institute of Physics. "Physics Success Stories." Available online. URL: http://www.aip.org/success. Accessed on May 9, 2006. Examples of how the study of physics has impacted society and technology.

American Physical Society. "Physics Central." Available online. URL: http://www.physicscentral.com. Accessed on May 9, 2006. A collection of articles, illustrations, and photographs explaining physics and its applications and introducing some of the physicists who are advancing the frontiers of physics even further.

American Society for Microbiology. "How Thermophiles Survive Extreme Heat." Available online. URL: http://www.microbe.

org/microbes/thermophiles.asp. Accessed on May 9, 2006. Explains how the molecules of heat-loving microorganisms have adapted to extreme temperatures.

Equine Center, The. "Thermography." Available online. URL: http://www.theequinecenter.com/thermography.htm. Accessed on May 9, 2006. Explains the use of thermography in veterinary medicine.

Environmental Protection Agency (EPA). "Global Warming." Available online. URL: http://www.epa.gov/globalwarming/kids. Accessed on May 9, 2006. The EPA is a United States government agency devoted to studying and protecting the environment. This Web site is intended for young students and explores the topic of global warming.

Environmental Protection Agency (EPA). "Heat Island Site." Available online. URL: http://www.epa.gov/hiri/index.html. Accessed on May 9, 2006. A collection of web pages that explains the phenomenon of higher temperatures in cities and discusses potential solutions to reduce or curb the problem.

Exploratorium: The Museum of Science, Art and Human Perception. Available online. URL: http://www.exploratorium.edu. Accessed on May 9, 2006. An excellent Web resource containing much information on the scientific explanations of everyday things.

Haynes, Leland R. "SR-71 Blackbirds." Available online. URL: http://www.wvi.com/~sr71webmaster/sr-71~1.htm. Accessed on May 9, 2006. A huge quantity of information on one of the fastest vehicles in the world, collected and maintained by a retired United States Master Sergeant.

HowStuffWorks, Inc., homepage. Available online. URL: http://www.howstuffworks.com. Accessed on May 9, 2006. Contains a large number of articles, generally written by knowledgeable authors, explaining the science behind everything from computers to satellites.

National Aeronautics and Space Administration (NASA) homepage. Available online. URL: http://www.nasa.gov. Accessed on May 9, 2006. News and information from the United States agency devoted to the exploration of space and the development of aerospace technologies. This Web site contains a huge number of resources, including photographs, movies, and clear and accurate explanations of the science of space exploration.

National Institute of Standards and Technology (NIST). "NIST-F1 Cesium Fountain Atomic Clock." Available online. URL: http://tf.nist.gov/timefreq/cesium/fountain.htm. Accessed on May 9, 2006. NIST is a government agency whose mission is to develop and apply accurate methods of measurement, including the measurement of time. This Web page explains an atomic clock, the NIST-F1, which is the most accurate clock in the world.

Nave, Carl R. "HyperPhysics Concepts." Available online. URL: http://hyperphysics.phy-astr.gsu.edu/hbase/hph.html. Accessed on May 9, 2006. This comprehensive resource for students offers illustrated explanations and examples of the basic concepts of all the branches of physics, including heat and thermodynamics.

NOVA Online. "Time Travel." Available online. URL: http://www.pbs.org/wgbh/nova/time. Accessed on May 9, 2006. This Web site is a companion to an episode of *NOVA* that explores the possibility of time travel. *NOVA* is a popular PBS television series consisting of documentaries on a variety of science and technology topics.

Stern, David P. "Seasons of the Year." Available online. URL: http://www-spof.gsfc.nasa.gov/stargaze/Sseason.htm. Accessed on May 9, 2006. Illustrated account of the seasons, with links to related topics including latitude and longitude, sundials, and navigation.

INDEX

Italic page numbers indicate illustrations.

A

absolute (Kelvin) scale 7, 67, 79
absolute time 111
absolute zero 7–8, 67–70, *68,* 79
absorption of heat, by urban structures 23–24
acceleration 88, 102
activity, heat and 56
adaptation, to warm/ cold environment 38
aerogel 11
aerosols 25
afterburner 96, 98
air 11, 43, 82, 89–90
air conditioner x, 25, 46, 60–65, *63*
aircraft, jet-powered. *See* jet airplanes
airliners, commercial 95
albedo 24, 25
alternating current, for clock power 110
amino acids 127
ammonia 126
amplitude, of pendulum motion 107
analog thermometer 5
angle of incidence *20,* 20–21, *22*

animals. *See* living things
Archaea 50
asbestos 11
atmosphere. *See* global warming; greenhouse effect
atomic bonds 36
atomic clock 110, 112, 120
atoms *3,* 3–4, 110
automobile
    crash *113*
    greenhouse effect on interior of 28, 35
    internal combustion engine 82–92, *83, 84, 89*
    jet-powered 92
    radiator 58
    steam-powered 79–80
axis, rotational. *See* rotational axis, of Earth

B

babies, heat loss in 12
Back to the Future (film) 121
bacteria, freezing to halt growth of 52
ball, rubber 114
basking, by ectothermic animals 40–41
bats 42
Bell X-1 71

Benjamin Franklin Bridge *12*
"big bang" 70, 122
bimetal thermometer 6
biology. *See* living things
birds 43
black hole 120–121
Black Rock Desert 92
blood, body temperature maintenance by 45
blower (supercharger) 90
blubber 44
blue star 6
body temperature 31–53
body temperature, of humans 32–35
boiler, steam engine 73, 75
boiling point, of water 7, 16
bouncing balls 114, 118
brass, as heat conductor 36
bridges 11, 18, 19

C

caiman *39*
calendar 102–103
California, SS 79
Camaro SS-350 87–88
capsaicin 38
car. *See* automobile
carbohydrates 40
carbon dioxide 29

Carnot, Sadi ix, 77–79
Carnot engine 77–79, 100, 125
Carnot's theory 77–79
  and efficiency of heat engines 116, 118
  and efficiency of jet engines 95
  and entropy 114, 116, 118
  and internal combustion engine 85
car radiator 58
celestial navigation 109
cell (biology) 49, 52
Celsius, Anders 6
Celsius temperature scale (°C) 6, 7, 67
cesium atom 110
CFC (chlorofluorocarbon) 64
chemical reactions 31, 32, 49–50
Chevrolet Camaro SS-350 87–88
children, heat loss in 12
chili peppers 38
chlorine 64
chlorofluorocarbon (CFC) 64
cities, as heat islands 23–26, 24
climate change, global 26–30
clock 102–110, 105, 108
clothing, thermal effect of 43–44
cold, sensation of 35–38
cold-blooded animals 40–41. See also warm-blooded/cold-blooded animals
cold spots 47, 48
cold water, effect on fish 41
combustion 71, 85
combustion chamber, jet engine 93–94, 94
compression ratio 88–91, 89

compressor
  air conditioning 63–64
  jet engines 94, 94, 95, 97–99
  supercharged engines 90
computer, cooling needs of 56
concrete, expansion of 18
condensation, in steam engine operation 75
condenser 64, 65
conduction 8, 14, 35, 37
conductors, of heat 10–11, 36
conformation (protein) 49–50
connecting rod 73, 74
conservation of energy, law of 39–40, 57
construction materials 23–25
control, of temperature 56–60
convection 9
convection current
  in air 11
  computer cooling 56
  effect on human body temperature 43
  engine cooling 58
  power plants cooling 58–59
  in water 11–12
  wind 45
core temperature, of human body 33, 44, 47
cosmology 123
crankshaft 73, 74, 82, 86–87
crude oil 85
cruise ship 81
cryonics 52–53
cylinders, of internal combustion engine 82–84

D
"dark energy" 124
death 52–53
degree, in Fahrenheit/Celsius temperature scales 7
diesel engines 90
digital thermometer 5
dilation of time 112
dinosaurs 42
direction, of time 112–114
Discovery (space shuttle) 36
disorder, entropy and 114–118
displacement, engine 87–88, 91
DNA 52, 127

E
Earth 30
  global warming 26–30
  radiation, conduction, and convection on 13
  rotational axis 21
  rotation of 102–103
  seasons 19–23
  as sink for heat pumps 66–67
  temperature of x
"Earth time" 119
ectothermy 39
efficiency
  of Carnot engine 79
  of heat engine 77, 78
  of internal combustion engine 85–86
  of jet engines 95, 96
  of steam engine 76
Egypt, ancient 102
Einstein, Albert 111–112, 118, 120
Einstein-Rosen bridge 121
electrical current 56, 61, 64
electrical power plants. See power plants, electrical

electric motor, electric
    generator *vs.* 114
electromagnetic radia-
    tion 9, 9–10
electromagnetism 114
electrons, heat conduc-
    tion and 36
elephant 58, *59*
El Niño 15
endothermy 39, 40
energy
    and air conditioning
        x, 60–61, 64
    and entropy 126
    flow of 8–14, *9, 10*
    heat as ix
    and heat pumps 66
    horsepower 86
    in iceberg 4–5
    and self-organization
        126–127
    for steam engine
        boiler 75
    thermodynamics
        and 2
    work and 2
energy conversion, body
    heat and 39–40
energy transformations
    57, 61
entropy 114–118, *115*
    and efficiency of
        heat engine 77
    and end of universe
        124
    and evolution of uni-
        verse 123
    and origins of life
        126–127
    and second law of
        thermodynamics
        117
environment 1–30, 79
environmental science
    48, 59
enzyme 49, 52
escapement 104–106,
    105
Eskimos 11
evaporator (air condi-
    tioning) 61–63

exhaust 86, 90
exhaust valve 82
exothermic reaction 85
expansion
    of freezing water 52
    thermal. *See* thermal
        expansion
    of universe 122, 124
expansion joints 19
external combustion
    engine 81. *See also*
    steam engine
Exxon-Valdez oil spill
    43

F
F-15 fighter jet 97
F/A-22 Raptor jet fighter
    98, *98*
Fahrenheit, Gabriel 6
Fahrenheit temperature
    scale (°F) 6, 7, 67
fan 56, 95
fat 40, 44
feathers 43
fever 34–35
fire 46
first law of thermody-
    namics 57–59, 61,
    75–77, 79
fish 41
floors, sensation of hot
    and cold on 35
flow, of energy 8–14,
    9, 10
flow, of time 112–114
fluids. *See* liquids
flywheel 73, *74*
foliot and verge 104–
    106, *105*
food requirements (ecto-
    thermic animals) 41
Ford, Henry 82
Ford Mustang 88
Formula One cars
    90–92
fossils 126
four-stroke engine 82–
    84, *83*
freezing, of food 52

freezing point, of water
    7, 16
frequency 9, 107
friction
    first law of thermo-
        dynamics 57
    and heat 2–3, 56
    and limits of heat
        engine efficiency 78
    and pendulum
        motion 107
    in racing engines
        88, 91–92
    second law of ther-
        modynamics 62
    on surfaces of jet
        planes 97, 99
fuel-air mixture 89–90,
    94
fuel economy, of racing
    engines 92
fur 43

G
galaxies, expansion of
    122
Galileo Galilei 106, 107
gases 4, 61–64, 92–93
gasoline 82, 85
gas turbines 92–96, *94*
geothermal heat pump
    67
glaciers 26
glass 28
global warming 26–30
glowing objects, tem-
    perature of 5–6
Gordon, Jeff 71
gravestone *115*
gravitation 113–114,
    122–124
gravity 107, 120–121
Greece, ancient ix
greenhouse *27*, 27–28
greenhouse effect 27–28
greenhouse gases 29
Greenland 26
Gregorian calendar 103
grooming, by animals
    43

H
Harrison, John 109
head, thermal sensitivity of 45
heat. *See also* kinetic energy
  absolute zero 67–70
  absorption by urban structures 23–24
  and body temperature 31–53
  conductors and insulators 36
  cooling down/heating up 14–19
  created by urban activity 25
  early harnessing of ix
  early view as fluid 2
  from electrical current 56
  and entropy 116, 118
  and the environment 1, 1–30
  everyday usage of term 2
  extreme temperatures and life 49–53, 51
  first law of thermodynamics 57–59, 61, 75–77, 79
  flow of energy 8–14, 9, 10
  global warming 26–30
  and muscles 40
  production by motion 56
  refrigerators and air conditioners 60–65
  relationship to motion 2–5
  reversible heat pumps 65–67
  seasons of the year 19–23, 20, 22
  second law of thermodynamics 62
  sensation of hot and cold 31–53
  and technology 55–70
  and temperature and 2–8
  temperature control 56–60
  thermography 47–48
  transfer of. *See* heat transfer
  urban heat islands 23–26, 24
  waste, in internal combustion engine 86
  and work 76–77
heat capacity 15–17, 58
heat engine 71–100, 72, 76
  automobile engines 82–92, 83, 84, 89
  Carnot engine 78–79
  and entropy 114
  future developments 96–100, 98
  jet engines/gas turbines 92–96, 94, 96
  passenger car engine 82–88
  racing engines 88–92
  steam power 72–81, 74, 80
  and thermodynamics 125
heat flow 14, 116
heating/cooling of objects 14–19
heat islands 23–26, 24
heat pumps 65–67
heat-seeking missiles 98
"heat signature" 98
heat sink 60, 66–67, 79
heatstroke 35
heat transfer 8, 14–19
  and air conditioning 60
  on bridges 11
  effect on astronauts in space 13
  and sensation of hot and cold 35
  and temperature changes 14
  for temperature control of machines 56–60
  and Thermos bottle 13–14
hertz (cycles per second) 107
Hertz, Heinrich 107
high-speed trains 19
home design, for cooling 46, 46
horsepower 86
horses, pollution from 80
"hot" (spicy) food 38
hot spots 47, 48
hourglass 104
house, heat regulation design 46
Howard, Luke 23
human activity, greenhouse effect and 29
humans, heat and 32–38, 42–43
hurricanes, effect of global warming on 26–27
Huygens, Christiaan 107
hydrofluorocarbon 64
hydrogen 99, 126
hydrothermal vents 50, 51
hyperthermia 34–35, 44–45
hypothalamus 34
hypothermia 34

I
IC (integrated circuit) chips 56

ice 18, 52, 55
iceberg 1, *1*, 4–5, 17–18
ideal gas law 63
ideal heat engine. *See*
    Carnot engine
igloo 11
immune system 35
industrial activity 29
Industrial Revolution
    ix, 71, 73, 79
infrared detector 47
infrared goggles 12
infrared images *13*
infrared radiation 10,
    28, 48
insulation 33, 40
insulator. *See* thermal
    insulator
intake valve 82
integrated circuit (IC)
    chips 56
internal combustion
    engine 58, 81–93, *83,
    84, 89,* 100
internal energy 57
isolated systems 117,
    123

J
jet airplanes *93,* 95,
    97, 98
jet engine 92–96, *96*
Joule, James 76–77

K
Kelvin, Lord 6
Kelvin temperature scale
    (K). *See* absolute scale
kerosene 85
kinetic energy 3–5, 36,
    57

L
lake, thermal pollution
    of 59
land, heat capacity of
    15
land speed record 92
latent heat 16–17, *17,*
    44–45, 75

laws of physics
    and birth of universe
    123
    symmetry in x–xi
    time and 110–114,
    113, 122
layers, dressing in
    43–44
leap year 103
life, origin of 125–127
light, and temperature of
    stars 5–6
light, speed of 111–112
lipids 49. *See also* fat
liquids 4, 64–66
living things, body tem-
    perature of 31–53, *51*
longitude 109
Los Angeles, California
    24

M
mackerel shark 41
mammals. *See* warm-
    blooded animals
marine animals 44
Mars 28
mass, heat capacity and
    16
Mauretania, RMS 81
measurement, of time
    102–110
medicine 47–48, 52
membrane, cell 52
menthol 38
mercury (element) 5
Mercury (planet) 28–29
metabolism 50
metals 6, 18, 35–37
methane 29, 126
microorganisms 50
Miller, Stanley 126–127
Model T 82
molecular motion *3,*
    7–8, 32
molecules, kinetic
    energy of 3–5
Moon 102
motion 2–5, 56. *See also*
    Newton's second law

of motion; Newton's
    third law of motion
muffler 82
muscle cars 88
muscles 40, 44

N
NASCAR 91, *91*
National Aeronautics
    and Space Adminis-
    tration (NASA) 99
navigation 109
Newcomen, Thomas 73
Newton's second law of
    motion 88, 102
Newton's third law of
    motion 92–93
North Atlantic Ocean
    34
Northern Hemisphere
    20, 21
nuclear power plants 81

O
oceans 15, 26
odors, spread of 116
oil 43
oil refining 85
oil spills 43
Onnes, Heike Kamer-
    lingh 69
orbit, of Earth 20
orbital plane, of Earth
    21
order, entropy and 114–
    118, 126–127
organic molecules 127
oscillation 110
oscillator, pendulum as
    107
Otto, Nikolaus 84
oxygen 40, 82, 86, 90
ozone layer 64

P
parks, urban 25–26
particles, in urban air
    25
PCR (polymerase chain
    reaction) 52

pendulum 106, *106*, 106–107, *108*
period (pendulum motion) 107
periodicity, pendulums and *106*, 106–107
phase changes 15–18
phase transition 16–17, *17*, 45, 64
physics, laws of 110–114, *113*, 122, 123
piston 73, *74*, 82–84, 87–89
planetary motion 113–114
Planet of the Apes (film) 119
plant life 25
polar ice 26
pollution 23, 25, 48, 59, 86
polymerase chain reaction (PCR) 52
Porsche 90
power plants, electrical 58, 81, 94
power stroke 82, 85, 86
precipitation 25
pressure (steam engine) 75
protein 32–33, 41, 49–50, 127

Q

quantum mechanics 8
quartz crystal 110

R

racing engines 88–92, *91*
radiation. *See also* electromagnetic radiation
and absolute zero 69
and angle of incidence 20–21
detection by snakes 38
frequency change with temperature change *9*

heat transfer by Sun to Earth 19
heat transfer in space 13
radiational cooling 12
radiator, car 58, 86
railroad tracks, expansion/contraction of 19
rain 25
ramjet 98–99
reactant 49
receptors (biological) 37, 38
red star 6
refrigerator 65, 70, *76*
relativity 111–112
religion 125–126
remote sensing 47–48
reptiles. *See* cold-blooded animals
reversible heat pumps 65–67
river, thermal pollution of 59
rocket engine *72*
Rome, ancient 103
roofs, snow on 22
room temperature 33
rotational axis, of Earth 21
rpm (revolutions per minute) 86–87, 91–92
Rumford, Count 2–3
rural (definition) 23

S

sand clock 104
Savery, Thomas 72
science fiction 119, 121
scramjet 99–100
sea breeze 15
seasons 19–23, *20, 22*, 103
second law of thermodynamics 62
and air conditioning 61
and end of universe 124

and entropy 117, 118
and evolution of universe 123
and time 101
seizure 35
self-organization 126–127
shark 41
ships 79, 81, 94, 108–109
shivering 44
silica fiber 36
silver 36
singularity 120–122
skin temperature 33
snakes 38
snow 17, 22
solar radiation *10, 20, 22*
solar system 113–114
solids, molecular motion of 4
Southern Hemisphere 20, 21
Southern Oscillation 15
space 13, 69–70
spacecraft, future *119*
space shuttle 36
space travel, slowing of time during 119
spark plug 82
special theory of relativity 112
speed, of light 111–112
Spitzer Space Telescope 68
spontaneous process 116, 117
springs, for clock power 109–110
SR-71 reconnaissance jet 97, *97*
Stanley Steamer 79–80
stars 5–6, 120
statistics 117
steam engine 72–81, *74*
steam power 72–81
steamships 79
steam turbine *80*, 80–81

steel 18, 36
stellar evolution 120
sterilization, of surgical
   instruments 50
stream, thermal pollu-
   tion of 59
Styrofoam 11, 36
suburb 23
Sun
   angle of incidence to
      Earth 21
   effect on astronauts
      in space 13
   and greenhouses 28
   height in sky 21
   movement, as early
      timekeeper 102,
      103
   as source of energy
      for Earth 19
   temperature of 6
sundial 103
supercharger 90
superconductivity 69
supersonic flight 99
sweat gland 45
sweating 44–45
symmetry x–xi

T
tachometer 87
tailpipe 82
technology 42, 55–70
temperature
   and advanced jet air-
      craft 97–99
   changes with heat
      transfer 14
   core temperature, of
      human body 33
   of Earth x
   and frequency
      change of radia-
      tion 9
   and heat 2–8
   and kinetic energy of
      molecules 3–5
   life-forms in extreme
      temperatures 49–
      53, 51

   of living things
      31–53
   regulation of, in ani-
      mals and humans
      42–46, 46, 58, 59
   of stars 5–6
   in urban areas
      23–24
   using technology to
      control 56–60
temperature scales 6–8
tepid water 37–38
thermal energy 1, 71
thermal equilibrium
   14–15
   of Earth 67
   and greenhouse
      effect 28
   and insulators 37
   in space 70
   and thermometers
      37
thermal expansion
   in analog thermom-
      eter 5
   of heated materi-
      als 18
   in internal combus-
      tion engine 85
   of metals 6
   and pendulum
      motion 107
   of steel and concrete
      18
   of water 18
thermal imager 34
thermal insulator 11,
   33, 36, 36, 37, 44
thermal pollution 59
thermal sense, of
   humans 37–38
thermal tiles 36
thermodynamics 125–
   127. See also first law
   of thermodynamics;
   second law of thermo-
   dynamics; third law
   of thermodynamics;
   zeroth law of thermo-
   dynamics

   and air-conditioning
      60–61
   and dinosaurs 42
   effect on cities
      23–26
   and efficiency lim-
      its of heat engine
      100, 125
   and efficiency limits
      of steam engine 76
   and efficiency of jet
      engines 95
   and energy cost of
      cooling 70
   and global warming
      29–30
   and home design
      46, 46
   and racing cars 88
   root of term ix
   and skin tempera-
      ture 33
   and time 101
thermography 47–48
thermometer 5, 6, 37
thermophile 50
Thermos bottle 13–14
third law of thermody-
   namics 67, 69
Thompson, Benjamin
   (Count Rumford). See
   Rumford, Count
Thomson, William
   (Lord Kelvin). See
   Kelvin, Lord
thrust 94, 96
Thrust-SSC (Super-
   sonic Car) 92, 93
time x–xi, 101–124
   clocks 102–110,
      105, 108
   dilation of 112
   direction of 118
   entropy and disorder
      114–118, 115
   flow of 112–114
   and laws of physics
      110–114, 113, 122
   measurement of
      102–110

second law of ther-
modynamics 117
symmetry in xi
traveling in 118–122
universe, begin-
ning and end of
122–124
time travel 118–122
Titanic, RMS 18, 34, 81
Titan IV Centaur rocket
72
Tokyo, Japan 24, 25
trains 19, 79
transformation of
energy. *See* energy
transformations
tropical fish 41
tuna 41
tuning fork 110
turbine. *See* gas turbine;
steam turbine
turbocharger 90
two-stroke engine
84–85

U
ultraviolet radiation 64
United States, SS 81
universe, beginning and
end of 122–124
urban (derivation of
word) 23
urbanization 27
Urey, Harold 126–127

V
vacuum 13–14, 69
valves, engine 73, 82

vaporization, latent heat
of 75
velocity 102
V engine 84, *84*
Venus 28
verge. *See* foliot and
verge
veterinary medicine 48
volcanic vent 50

W
warm-blooded/cold-
blooded animals
39–42
waste, in conversion of
heat to work 77, 114
watch, electric 110
water
boiling point of 7, 16
as component of
cells 49
consumption by
sweating 45
convection currents
in 11–12
cooling of power
plants 58–59
freezing point of 7,
16
heat capacity of 15
and hypothermia 34
as percentage of
human body 49
tepid 37–38
thermal expansion
of 18
and Urey-Miller
experiment 126

water clock 104
water vapor 29, 73–75.
See also steam power
Watt, James 73, 76
weather 15, 23
wind, heat loss by 45
windchill factor 45
work
air-conditioning
61–63
and energy 2
first law of thermo-
dynamics 57
and heat 76–77
and heat engines
71
horsepower 86
internal combustion
engine 87
second law of ther-
modynamics 62
steam engine 76
wormhole 121
wristwatch 110

X
X-43A Hypersonic
Experimental Vehicle
98, 99

Y
Yeager, Chuck 71
year, exact length of
102–103

Z
zeroth law of thermody-
namics 14, 33, 35